Speed Racer™: The Next Generation

Volume 1

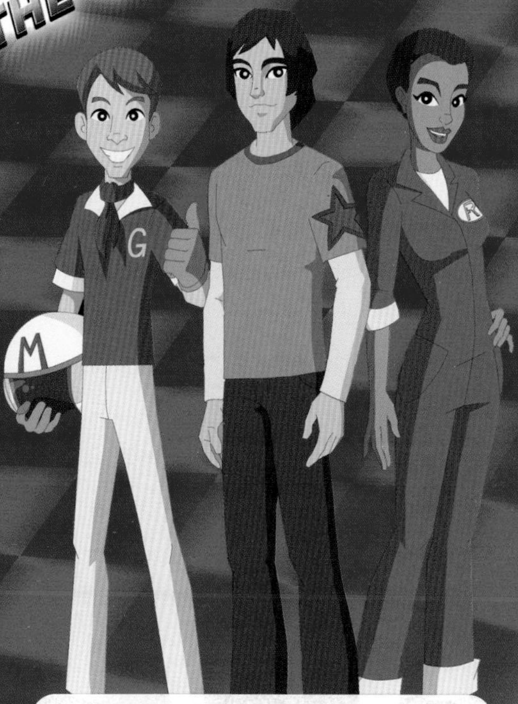
G
M
R

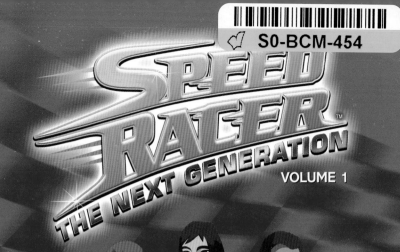

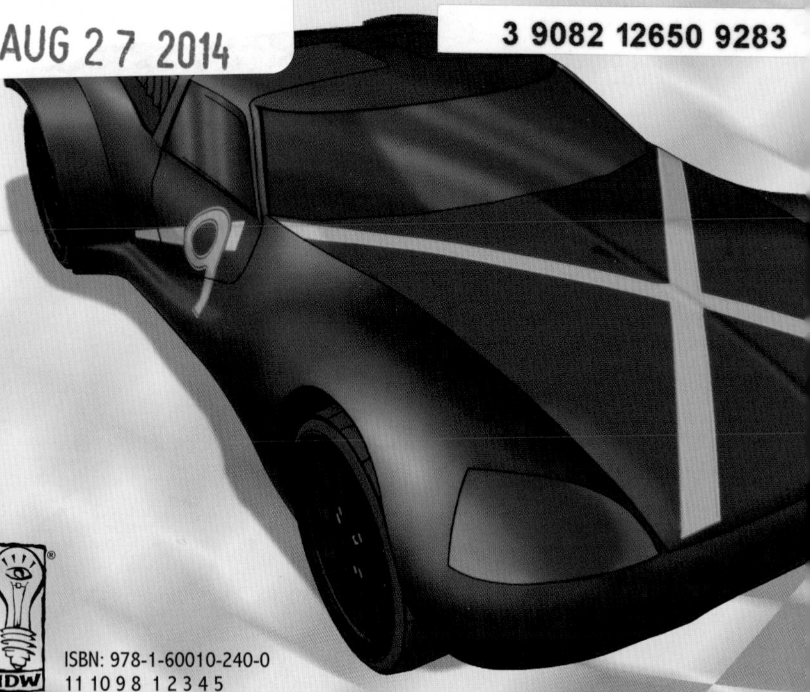

ISBN: 978-1-60010-240-0
11 10 9 8 1 2 3 4 5

Special thanks to Jim Rocknowski and Speed Racer Enterprises for their invaluable assistance.

IDW Publishing is:

Operations:
Moshe Berger, Chairman
Ted Adams, President
Matthew Ruzicka, CPA, Controller
Alan Payne, VP of Sales
Lorelei Bunjes, Dir. of Digital Services
Marci Kahn, Executive Assistant
Alonzo Simon, Shipping Manager

Editorial:
Chris Ryall, Publisher/Editor-in-Chief
Scott Dunbier, Editor, Special Projects
Andy Schmidt, Senior Editor
Justin Eisinger, Editor
Kris Oprisko, Editor/Foreign Lic.
Denton J. Tipton, Editor
Tom Waltz, Editor
Mariah Huehner, Assistant Editor

Design:
Robbie Robbins, EVP/Sr. Graphic Artist
Ben Templesmith, Artist/Designer
Neil Uyetake, Art Director
Chris Mowry, Graphic Artist
Amauri Osorio, Graphic Artist

Visit SPEED RACER @ www.speedracer.com

SPEED RACER: THE NEXT GENERATION ANIMATED, VOLUME 1. SEPTEMBER 2008. FIRST PRINTING.

“Origins, Parts 1 & 2”

Written by
Justin Gray and
James Palmiotti

Adaptation by
Zachary Rau

Collection Edits by
Justin Eisinger

Collection Design by
Tom B. Long

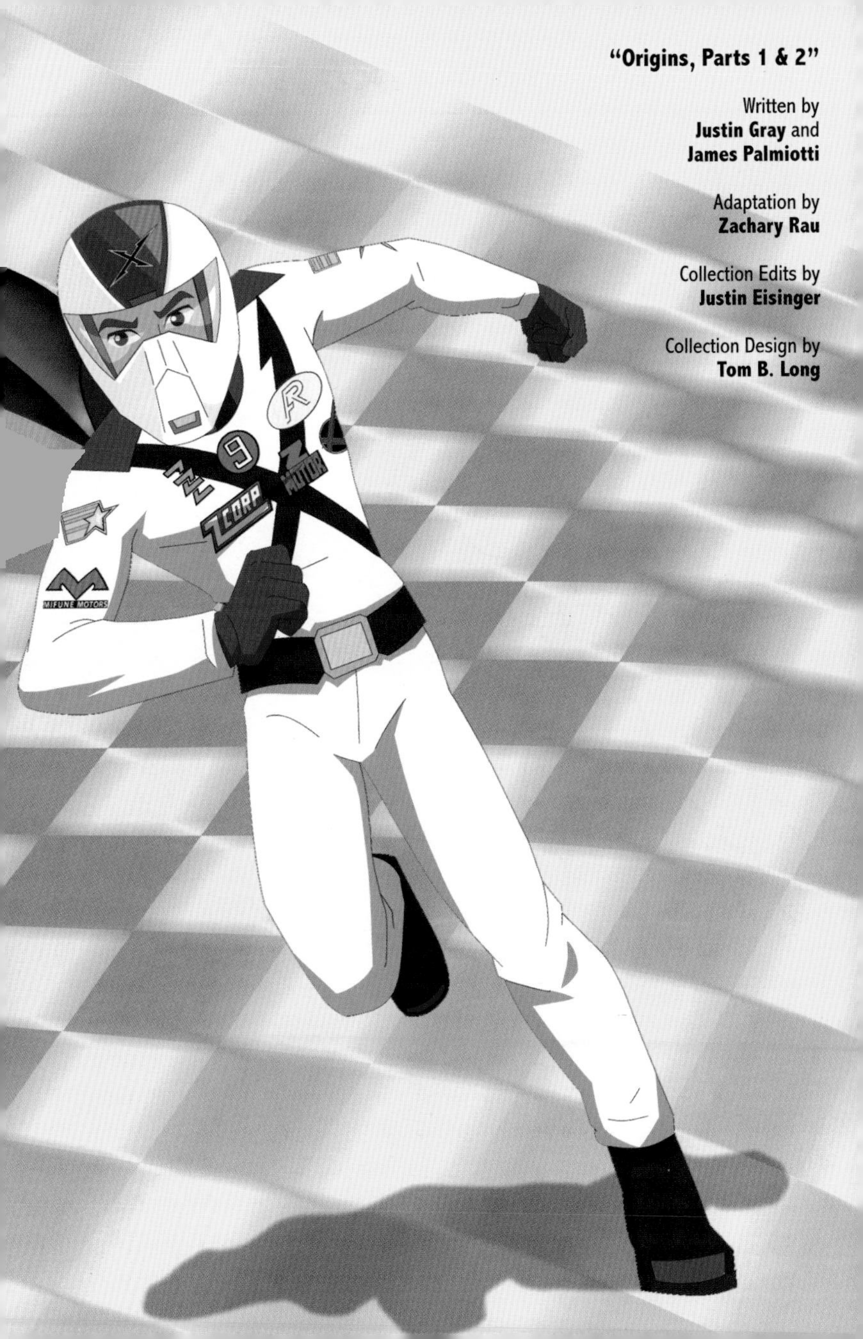

MIFUNE MOTORS
Z MOTOR
CORP
9

THE CREW

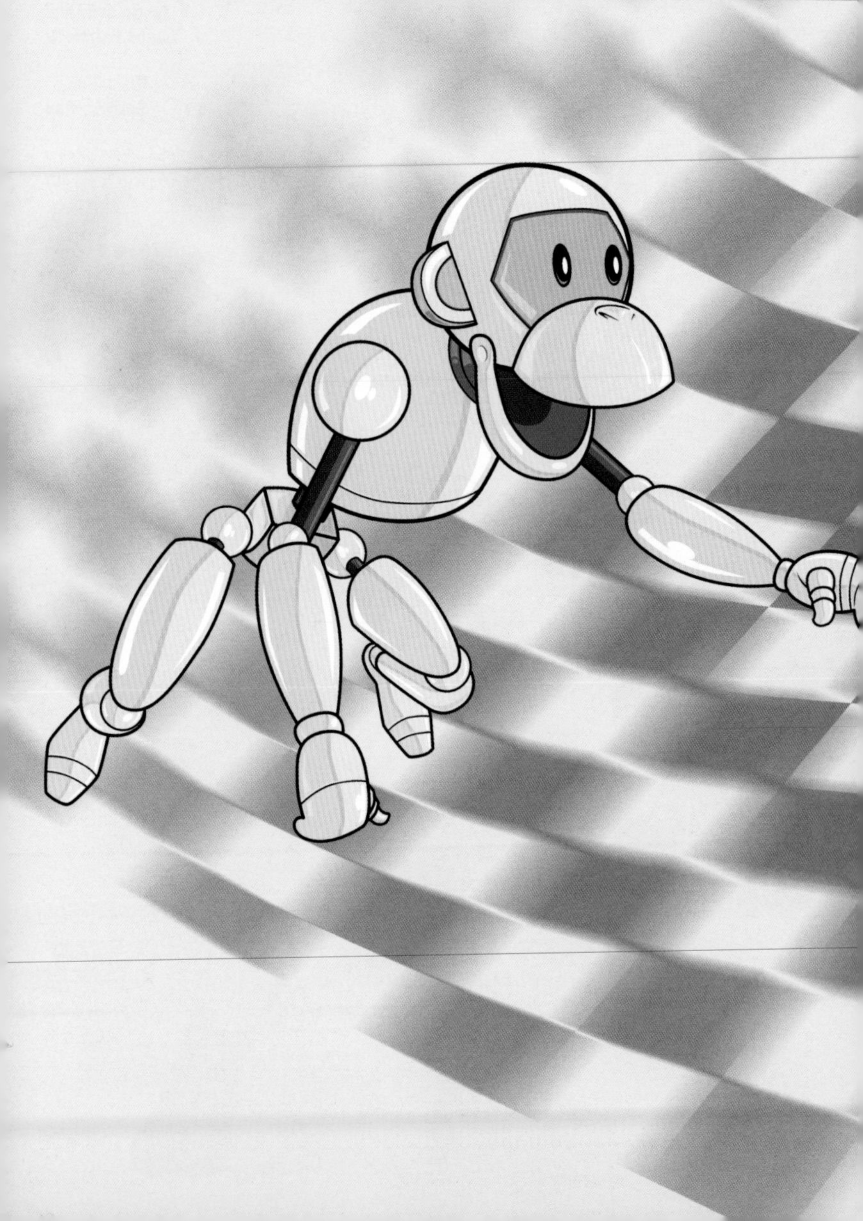

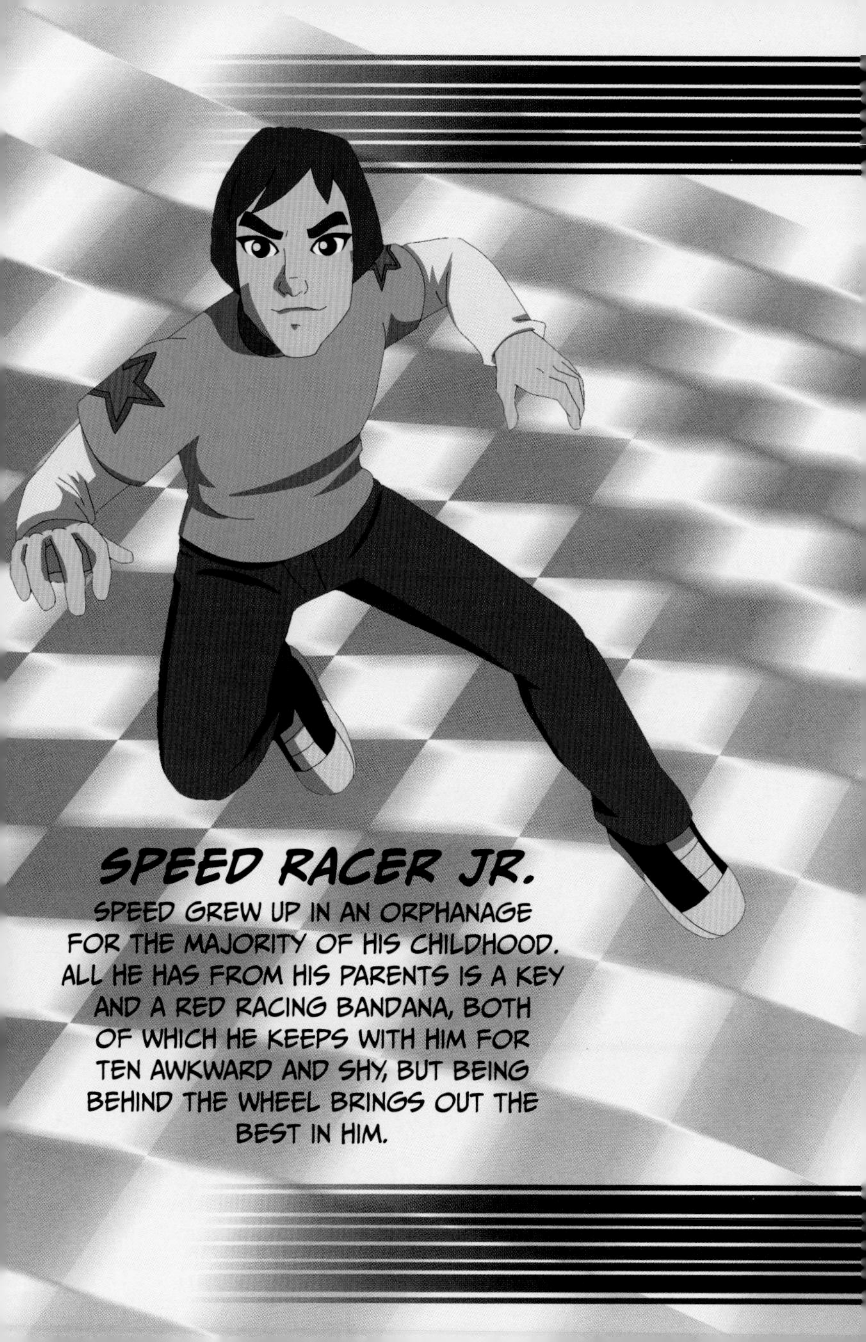

SPEED RACER JR.

SPEED GREW UP IN AN ORPHANAGE FOR THE MAJORITY OF HIS CHILDHOOD. ALL HE HAS FROM HIS PARENTS IS A KEY AND A RED RACING BANDANA, BOTH OF WHICH HE KEEPS WITH HIM FOR TEN AWKWARD AND SHY, BUT BEING BEHIND THE WHEEL BRINGS OUT THE BEST IN HIM.

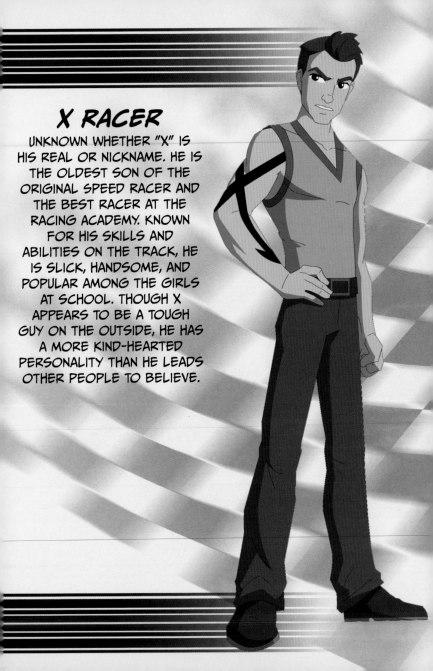

X RACER

UNKNOWN WHETHER "X" IS HIS REAL OR NICKNAME. HE IS THE OLDEST SON OF THE ORIGINAL SPEED RACER AND THE BEST RACER AT THE RACING ACADEMY. KNOWN FOR HIS SKILLS AND ABILITIES ON THE TRACK, HE IS SLICK, HANDSOME, AND POPULAR AMONG THE GIRLS AT SCHOOL. THOUGH X APPEARS TO BE A TOUGH GUY ON THE OUTSIDE, HE HAS A MORE KIND-HEARTED PERSONALITY THAN HE LEADS OTHER PEOPLE TO BELIEVE.

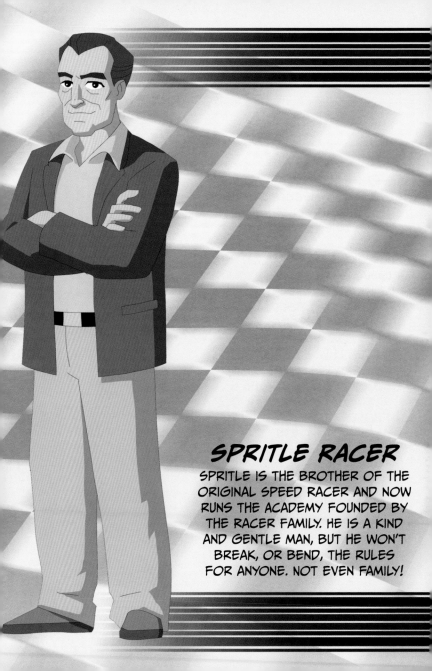

SPRITLE RACER

SPRITLE IS THE BROTHER OF THE ORIGINAL SPEED RACER AND NOW RUNS THE ACADEMY FOUNDED BY THE RACER FAMILY. HE IS A KIND AND GENTLE MAN, BUT HE WON'T BREAK, OR BEND, THE RULES FOR ANYONE. NOT EVEN FAMILY!

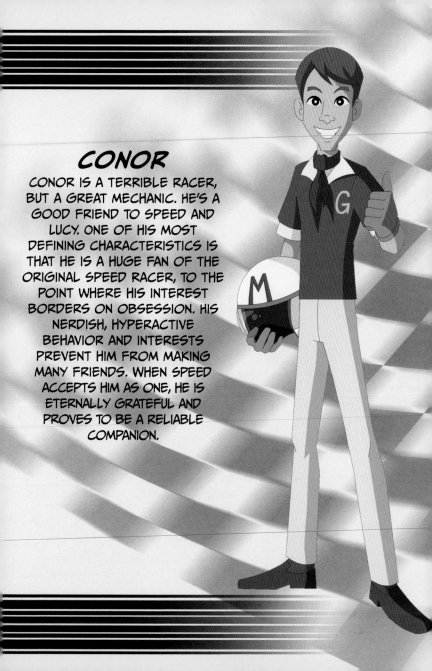

CONOR

CONOR IS A TERRIBLE RACER, BUT A GREAT MECHANIC. HE'S A GOOD FRIEND TO SPEED AND LUCY. ONE OF HIS MOST DEFINING CHARACTERISTICS IS THAT HE IS A HUGE FAN OF THE ORIGINAL SPEED RACER, TO THE POINT WHERE HIS INTEREST BORDERS ON OBSESSION. HIS NERDISH, HYPERACTIVE BEHAVIOR AND INTERESTS PREVENT HIM FROM MAKING MANY FRIENDS. WHEN SPEED ACCEPTS HIM AS ONE, HE IS ETERNALLY GRATEFUL AND PROVES TO BE A RELIABLE COMPANION.

CHIM-CHIM

CONOR BUILT THIS ROBOT
BASED ON THE ORIGINAL PET
CHIMPANZEE THE HEADMASTER
USED TO OWN, BUT ADDED
COUNTLESS GADGETS AND
PROFESSIONAL ENGINEERING
SKILLS. HE IS ENTIRELY LOYAL TO
CONOR, AND BY EXTENSION,
SPEED AND LUCY. CHIM-CHIM HAS
A SEEMINGLY UNLIMITED NUMBER
OF USES, FROM TRANSFORMING
INTO A SCOOTER, TO STORING
ANYTHING INSIDE THE
COMPARTMENT IN HIS STOMACH,
TO REPAIRING THE MACH SIX
WHILE IT'S MOVING. HOWEVER,
THAT DOESN'T STOP HIM FROM
EATING NECESSARY CAR PARTS,
OR CREATING THE USUAL KIND OF
MISCHIEF ALL MONKEYS MAKE.

LUCY

A GOOD FRIEND OF SPEED AND CONOR, LUCY IS THE SENSIBLE ONE OF THE GROUP. STRICT, OPEN-MINDED, AND STUDIOUS, SHE OFTEN ASSISTS CONOR WITH HIS WORK, BUT IS KNOWN TO BE A LITTLE BIT BOSSY AT TIMES. WHILE SHE IS GENERALLY A FRIENDLY AND CALM INDIVIDUAL, LUCY WILL OCCASIONALLY INSULT CONOR AND BOMBARD SPEED WITH CRITICISM. SHE ALWAYS MAKES UP FOR IT THOUGH BY HELPING HER FRIENDS.

ANNALISE ZAZIC

ANNALISE IS X'S GIRLFRIEND, AND THE SECOND BEST RACER IN THE SCHOOL. A SPOILED, SELFISH, WHINY MATERIAL GIRL, ANNALISE GETS WHATEVER SHE WANTS FROM HER FATHER, ZILE ZAZIC, SINCE THEY COME FROM A RICH FAMILY.

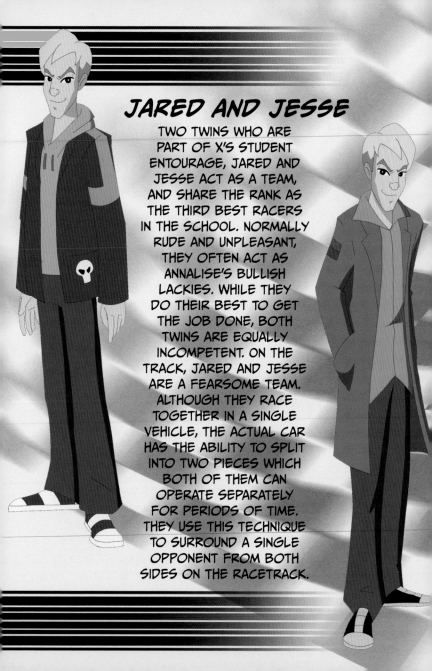

JARED AND JESSE

TWO TWINS WHO ARE PART OF X'S STUDENT ENTOURAGE, JARED AND JESSE ACT AS A TEAM, AND SHARE THE RANK AS THE THIRD BEST RACERS IN THE SCHOOL. NORMALLY RUDE AND UNPLEASANT, THEY OFTEN ACT AS ANNALISE'S BULLISH LACKIES. WHILE THEY DO THEIR BEST TO GET THE JOB DONE, BOTH TWINS ARE EQUALLY INCOMPETENT. ON THE TRACK, JARED AND JESSE ARE A FEARSOME TEAM. ALTHOUGH THEY RACE TOGETHER IN A SINGLE VEHICLE, THE ACTUAL CAR HAS THE ABILITY TO SPLIT INTO TWO PIECES WHICH BOTH OF THEM CAN OPERATE SEPARATELY FOR PERIODS OF TIME. THEY USE THIS TECHNIQUE TO SURROUND A SINGLE OPPONENT FROM BOTH SIDES ON THE RACETRACK.

ZILE ZAZIC

THE ACADEMY WOULD BE NOTHING WITHOUT ZILE ZAZIC— HE PAID FOR, DESIGNED, AND HAD THE ACADEMY'S RACING TRACK "BUILT FOR HIM." HE ALSO DONATED MANY BUILDINGS AND ADDITIONS TO THE SCHOOL, IS ON GREAT TERMS WITH THE HEADMASTER, AND VIEWS X AS THE STAR STUDENT OF THE SCHOOL. HOWEVER, HE HAS A VAGUE, MYSTERIOUS VENDETTA AGAINST SPEED RACER FROM LONG AGO.

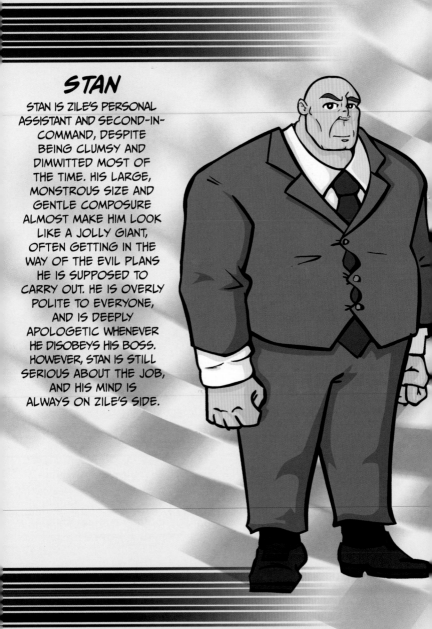

STAN

STAN IS ZILE'S PERSONAL ASSISTANT AND SECOND-IN-COMMAND, DESPITE BEING CLUMSY AND DIMWITTED MOST OF THE TIME. HIS LARGE, MONSTROUS SIZE AND GENTLE COMPOSURE ALMOST MAKE HIM LOOK LIKE A JOLLY GIANT, OFTEN GETTING IN THE WAY OF THE EVIL PLANS HE IS SUPPOSED TO CARRY OUT. HE IS OVERLY POLITE TO EVERYONE, AND IS DEEPLY APOLOGETIC WHENEVER HE DISOBEYS HIS BOSS. HOWEVER, STAN IS STILL SERIOUS ABOUT THE JOB, AND HIS MIND IS ALWAYS ON ZILE'S SIDE.

ARMAND ANISKOV

PROFESSOR ANISKOV IS AN INSTRUCTOR AT THE RACING ACADEMY WHO TEACHES THE CLASS ON OFFENSIVE DRIVING TECHNIQUES. STERN AND ALOOF, HE RARELY SHOWS ANY SIGNS OF FAVORITISM, AND TREATS ALL OF HIS STUDENTS WITH THE SAME AIR OF INDIFFERENCE. HE IS PROBABLY ONE OF THE MORE CRITICAL INSTRUCTORS THAT THE ACADEMY HAS TO OFFER, AND IS NOT PARTICULARLY WELL-LIKED BY ANY OF HIS STUDENTS BECAUSE OF THIS. HIS BEHAVIOR ALSO APPEARS TO SPREAD BEYOND THE STUDENT BODY, AS HE ONCE MADE A SNIDE REMARK TOWARDS HEADMASTER SPRITLE AFTER SPEED'S FIRST QUALIFYING RACE. THE STUDENTS OFTEN DESCRIBE HIM AS A MEAN PROFESSOR, PARTICULARLY CONOR.

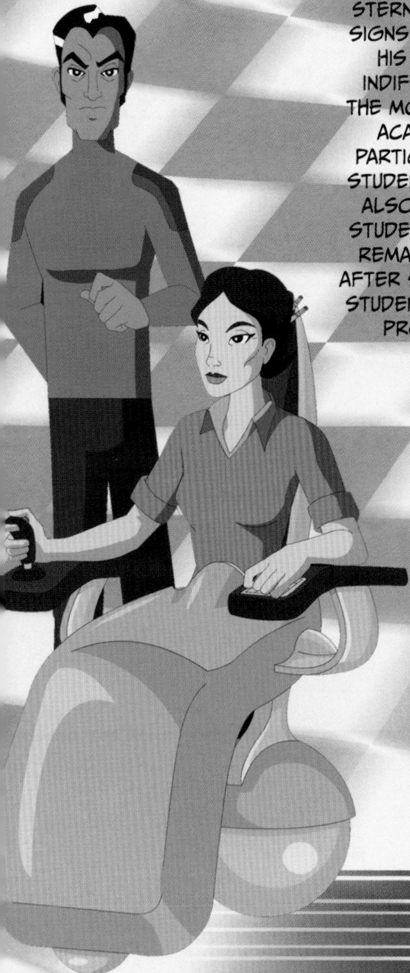

SUSAN WINN

SUSAN WINN IS AN INTELLIGENT AND LEVELHEADED WOMAN WHO TEACHES THE CLASS ON DEFENSIVE DRIVING TECHNIQUES AT THE RACING ACADEMY. SHE IS HANDICAPPED, AND TRAVELS AROUND IN A SLEEK, MOTORIZED WHEELCHAIR. PROFESSOR WINN IS GENERALLY MUCH KINDER AND MORE ACCEPTING OF HER STUDENTS THAN PROFESSOR ANISKOV, AND IS RESPECTED BECAUSE OF THIS. WHILE DISPLAYING A SENSE OF STRICT GUIDELINES AND ACCEPTABLE CONDUCT IN HER CLASSES, SHE IS A VERY FAIR INDIVIDUAL.

SPEED RACER™

THE NEXT GENERATION

ORIGINS

PART 1

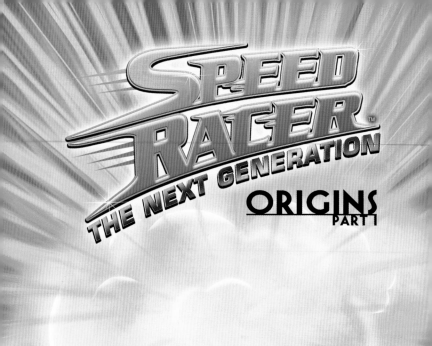

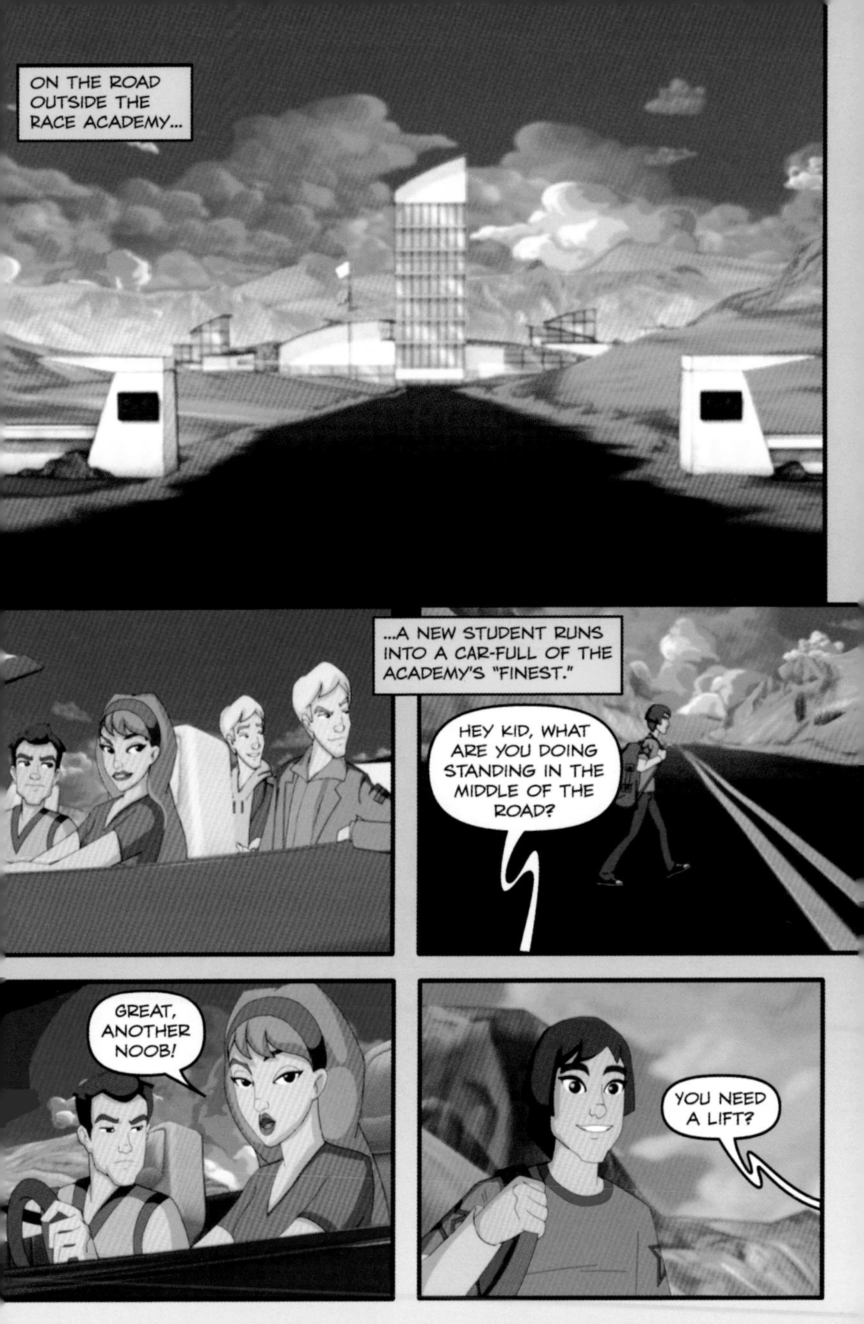
ON THE ROAD OUTSIDE THE RACE ACADEMY...
...A NEW STUDENT RUNS INTO A CAR-FULL OF THE ACADEMY'S "FINEST."
HEY KID, WHAT ARE YOU DOING STANDING IN THE MIDDLE OF THE ROAD?
GREAT, ANOTHER NOOB!
YOU NEED A LIFT?

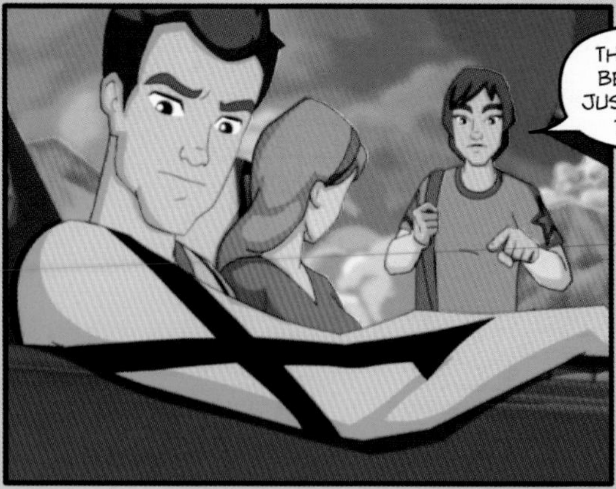
THAT WOULD BE GREAT, I JUST GOT OFF THE BUS.
HEY, YOU'RE X AREN'T YOU?

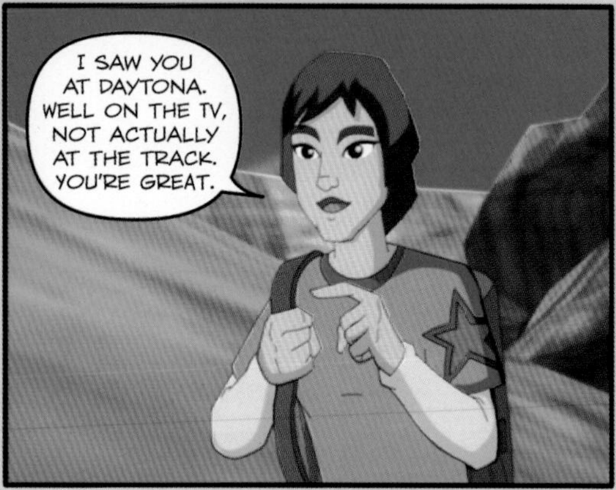
I SAW YOU AT DAYTONA. WELL ON THE TV, NOT ACTUALLY AT THE TRACK. YOU'RE GREAT.

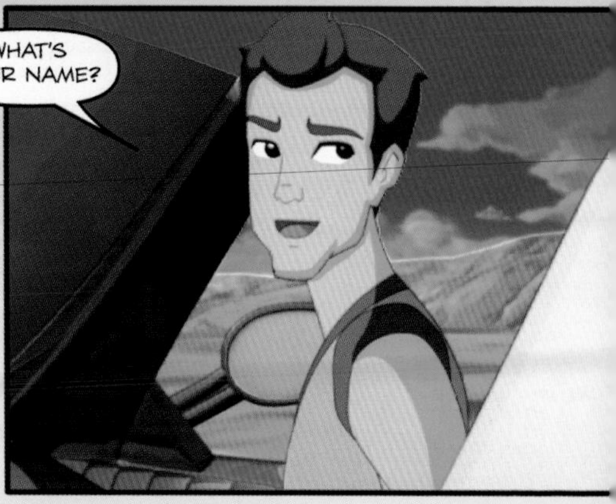
WHAT'S YOUR NAME?

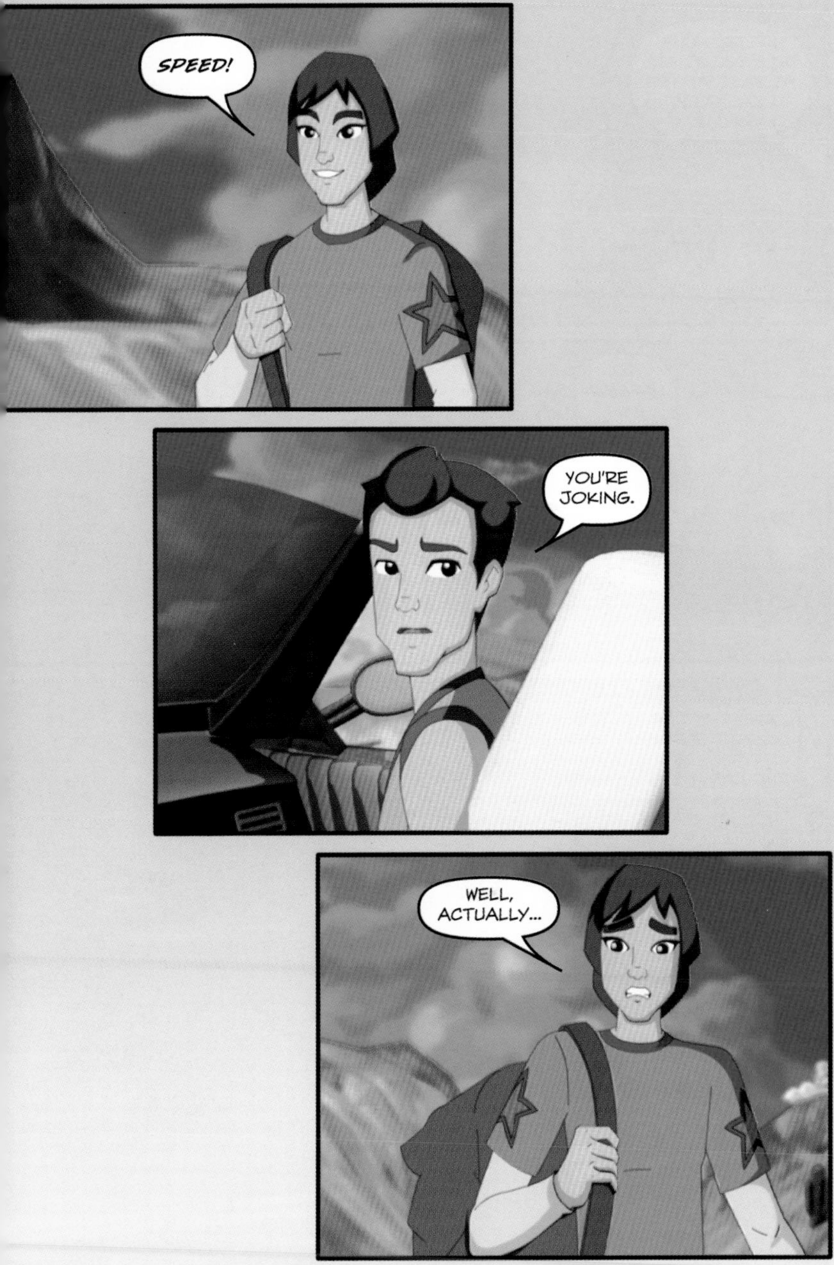
SPEED!
YOU'RE JOKING.
WELL, ACTUALLY...

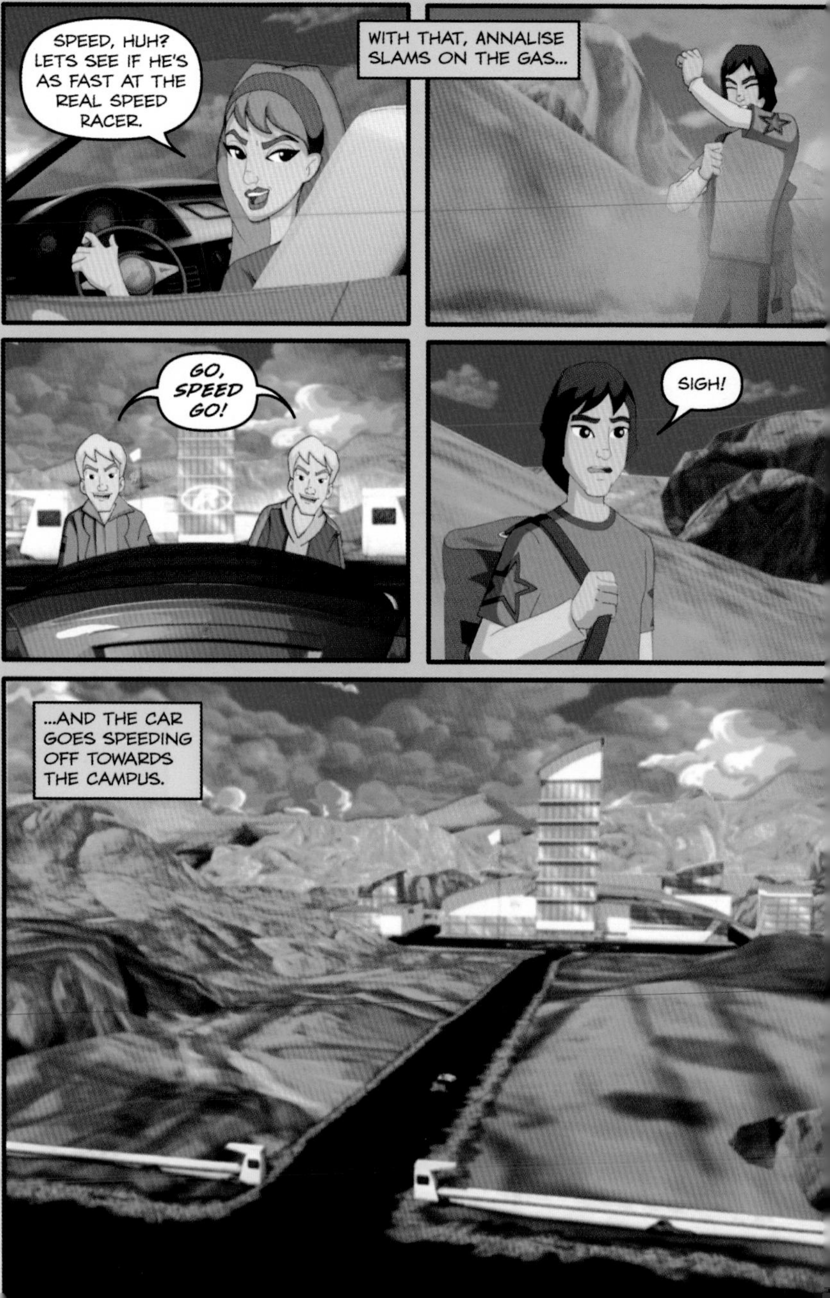
SPEED, HUH? LETS SEE IF HE'S AS FAST AT THE REAL SPEED RACER.
WITH THAT, ANNALISE SLAMS ON THE GAS...
GO, SPEED GO!
SIGH!
...AND THE CAR GOES SPEEDING OFF TOWARDS THE CAMPUS.

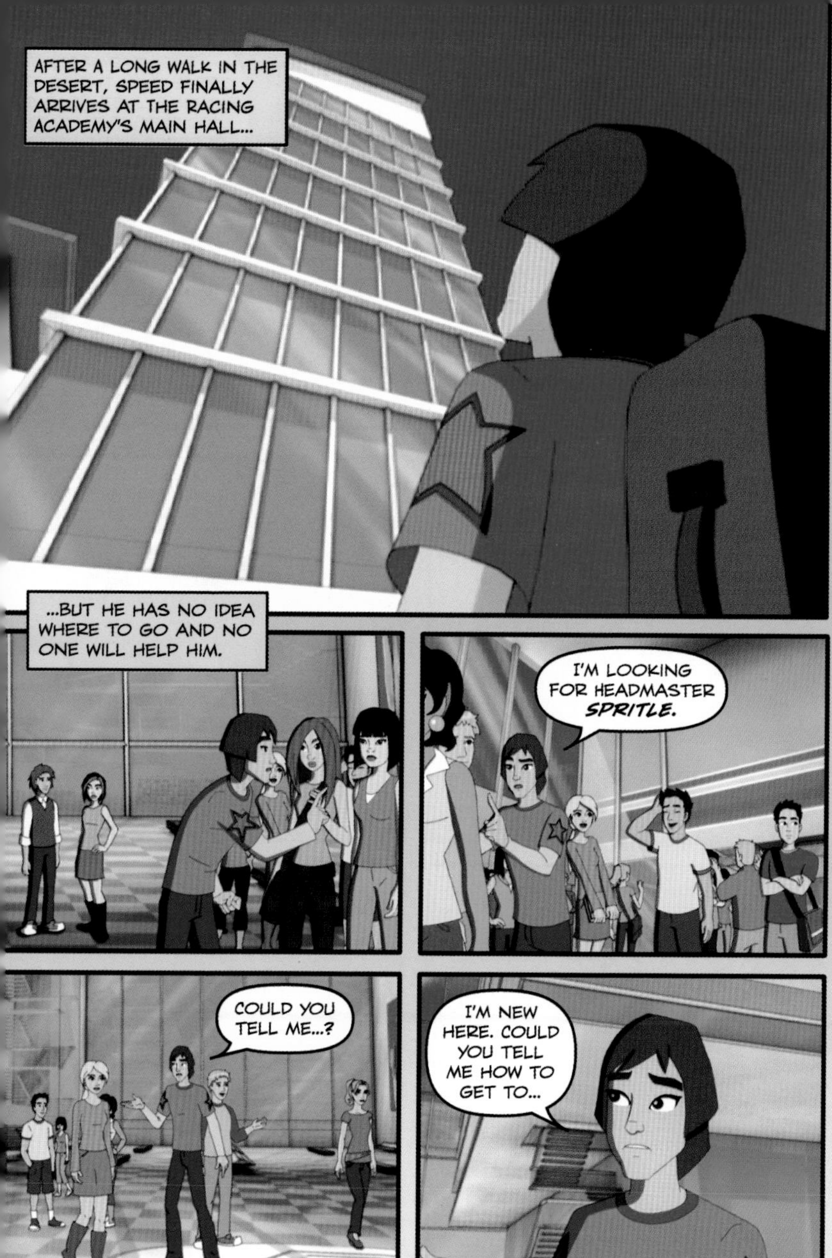
AFTER A LONG WALK IN THE DESERT, SPEED FINALLY ARRIVES AT THE RACING ACADEMY'S MAIN HALL...
...BUT HE HAS NO IDEA WHERE TO GO AND NO ONE WILL HELP HIM.
I'M LOOKING FOR HEADMASTER *SPRITLE.*
COULD YOU TELL ME...?
I'M NEW HERE. COULD YOU TELL ME HOW TO GET TO...

SPEED IS JUST ABOUT TO GIVE UP WHEN ONE STUDENT FINALLY SAVES HIM.

THE HEADMASTER'S OFFICE IS IN THE TOURISM BUILDING. JUST HEAD SOU 500 FEET, THEN TURN 3 DEGREES NORTH FOR 20 FEET, THEN MAKE A SHARP RIGHT.

WAIT, COULDN'T I JUST HEAD UP THAT PATH?

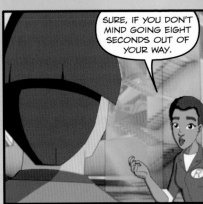

SURE, IF YOU DON'T MIND GOING EIGHT SECONDS OUT OF YOUR WAY.

UM, THANKS. I'M SPEED.

WAIT, DID YOU SAY YOUR NAME WAS SPEED? LIKE SPEED RACER?

UH... YEAH.

WOW, YOU SHOULDN'T BE TEASED AT ALL WITH THAT NAME! GOOD LUCK!

BY THE WAY, HAVE YOU SEEN A MONKEY AROUND HERE?

NO, BUT I'LL KEEP AN EYE OUT. WAIT, WHAT'S YOUR NAME?

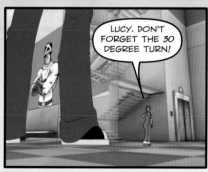

LUCY. DON'T FORGET THE 30 DEGREE TURN!

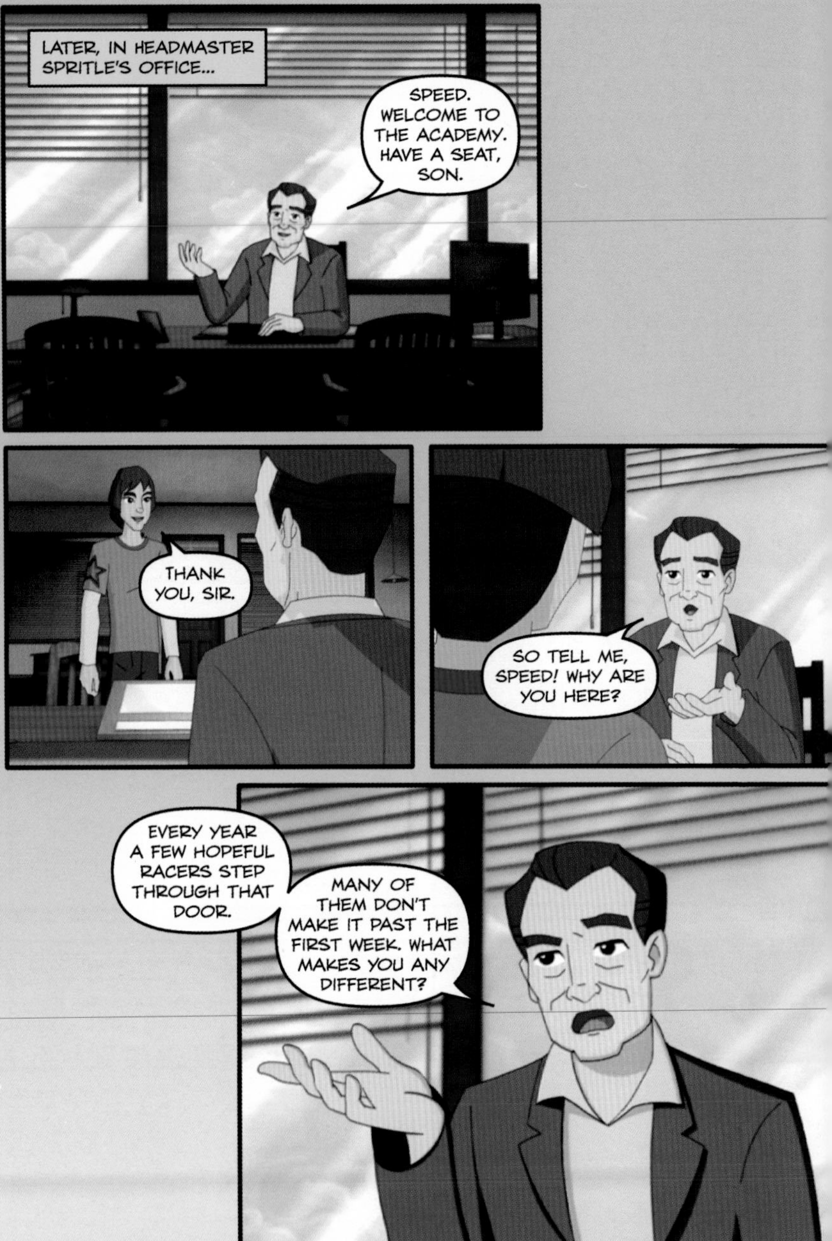
LATER, IN HEADMASTER SPRITLE'S OFFICE...
SPEED. WELCOME TO THE ACADEMY. HAVE A SEAT, SON.
THANK YOU, SIR.
SO TELL ME, SPEED! WHY ARE YOU HERE?
EVERY YEAR A FEW HOPEFUL RACERS STEP THROUGH THAT DOOR.
MANY OF THEM DON'T MAKE IT PAST THE FIRST WEEK. WHAT MAKES YOU ANY DIFFERENT?

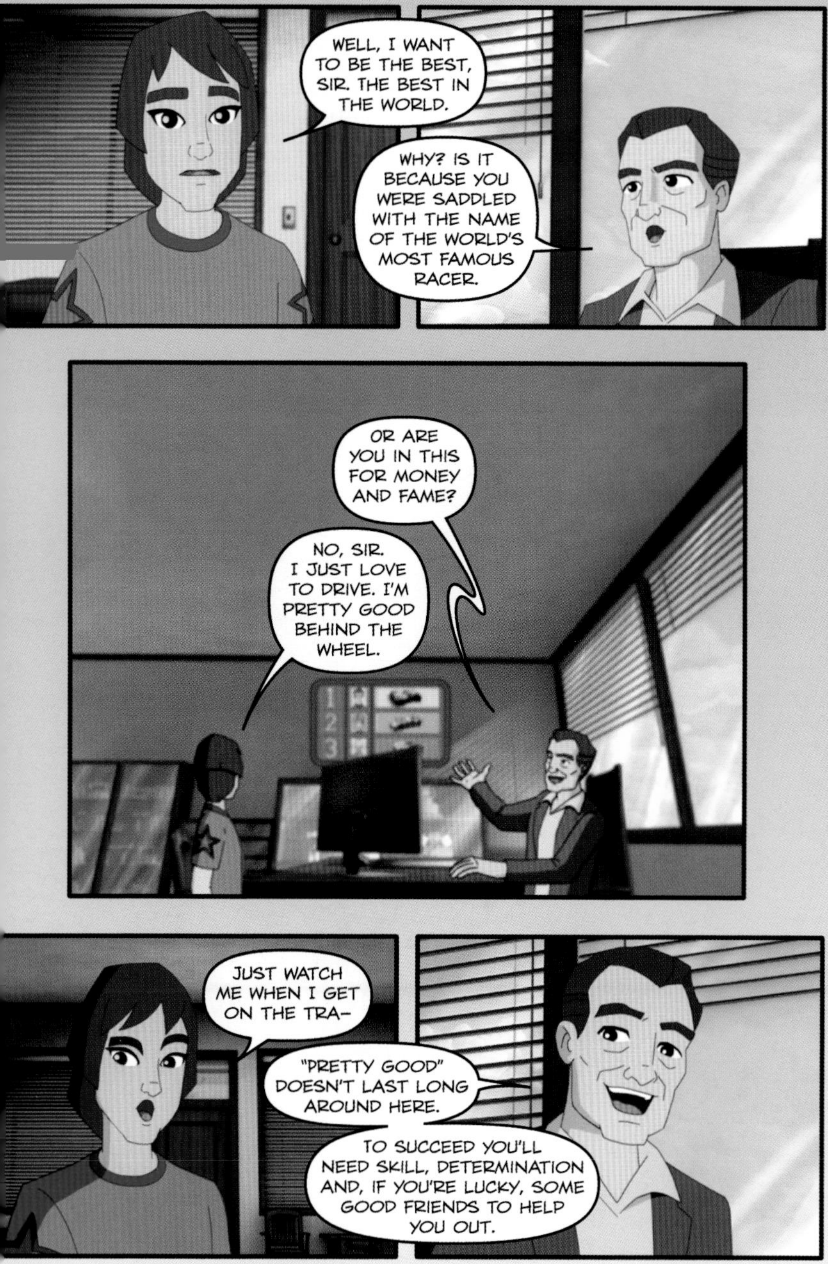
WELL, I WANT TO BE THE BEST, SIR. THE BEST IN THE WORLD.
WHY? IS IT BECAUSE YOU WERE SADDLED WITH THE NAME OF THE WORLD'S MOST FAMOUS RACER.
OR ARE YOU IN THIS FOR MONEY AND FAME?
NO, SIR. I JUST LOVE TO DRIVE. I'M PRETTY GOOD BEHIND THE WHEEL.
JUST WATCH ME WHEN I GET ON THE TRA–
"PRETTY GOOD" DOESN'T LAST LONG AROUND HERE.
TO SUCCEED YOU'LL NEED SKILL, DETERMINATION AND, IF YOU'RE LUCKY, SOME GOOD FRIENDS TO HELP YOU OUT.

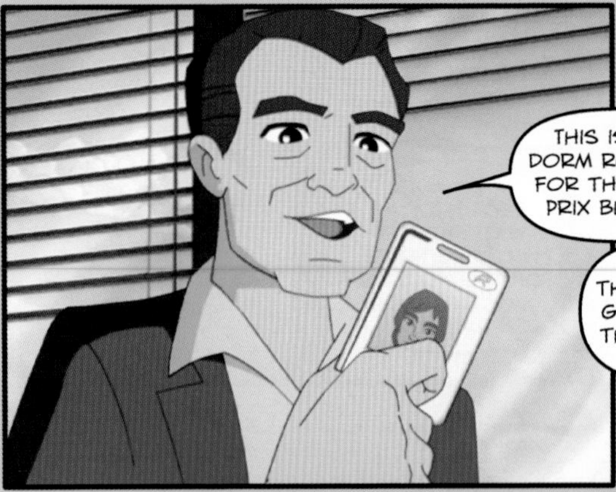
THIS IS YOUR DORM ROOM KEY FOR THE GRAND PRIX BUILDING.
DROP YOUR THINGS OFF AND GET READY FOR THE QUALIFYING RACE.

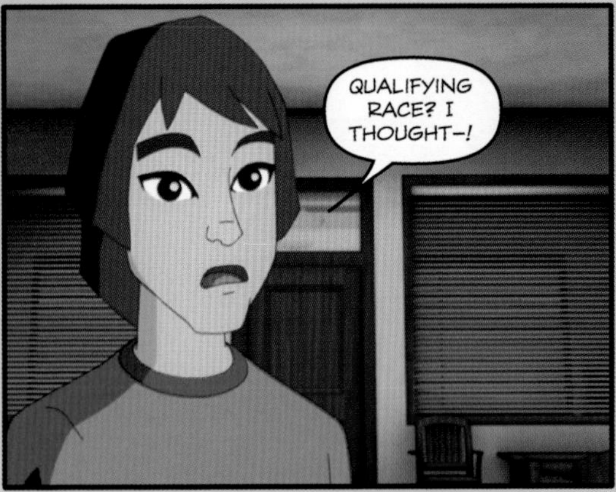
QUALIFYING RACE? I THOUGHT-!

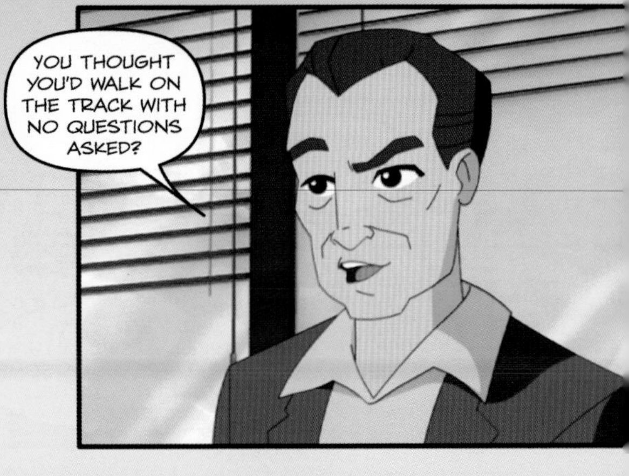
YOU THOUGHT YOU'D WALK ON THE TRACK WITH NO QUESTIONS ASKED?

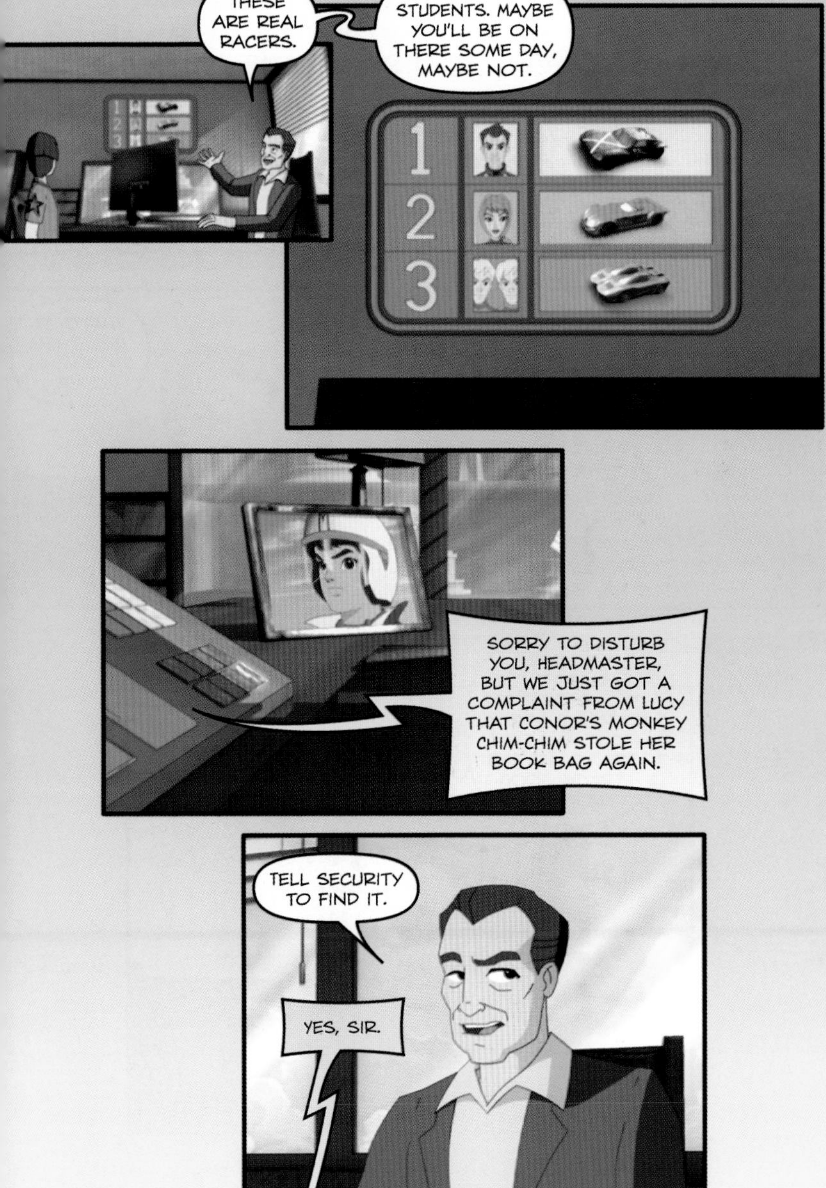
THESE ARE REAL RACERS.
OUR TOP STUDENTS. MAYBE YOU'LL BE ON THERE SOME DAY, MAYBE NOT.
1
2
3
SORRY TO DISTURB YOU, HEADMASTER, BUT WE JUST GOT A COMPLAINT FROM LUCY THAT CONOR'S MONKEY CHIM-CHIM STOLE HER BOOK BAG AGAIN.
TELL SECURITY TO FIND IT.
YES, SIR.

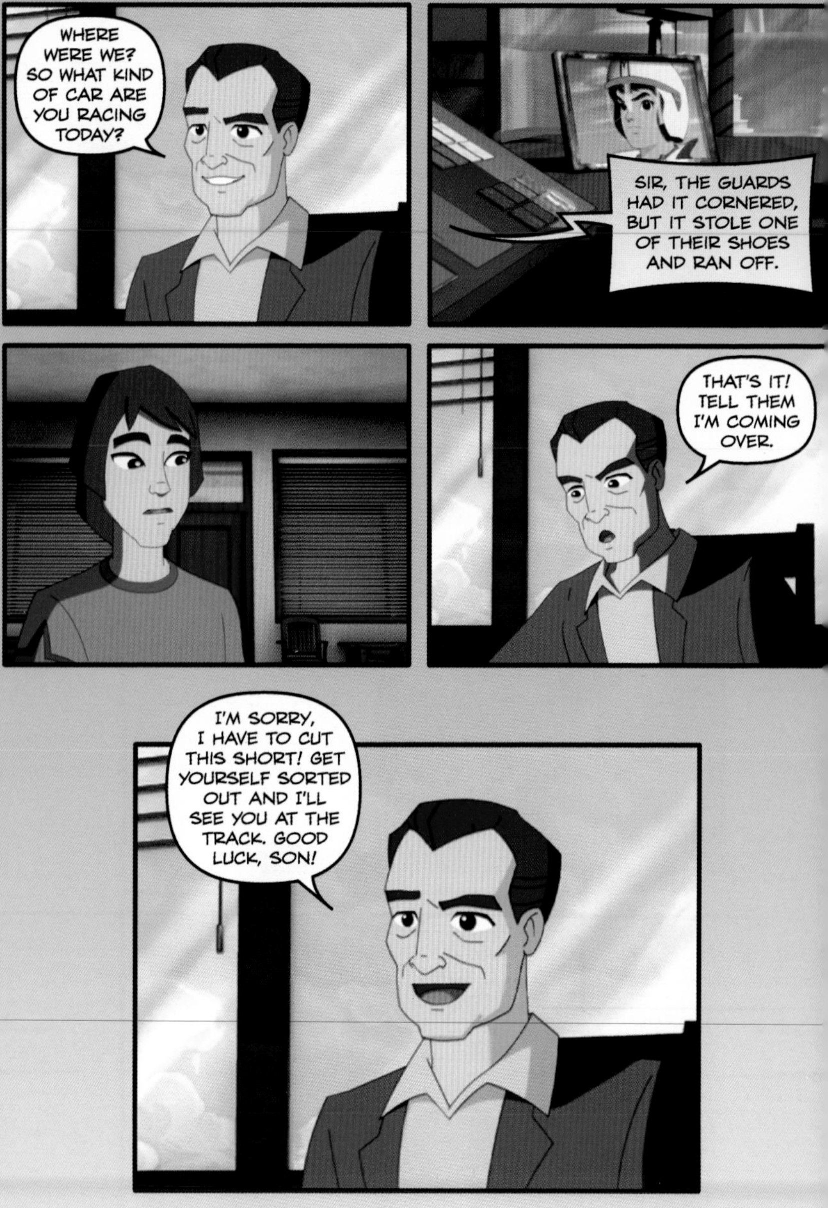
WHERE WERE WE? SO WHAT KIND OF CAR ARE YOU RACING TODAY?
SIR, THE GUARDS HAD IT CORNERED, BUT IT STOLE ONE OF THEIR SHOES AND RAN OFF.
THAT'S IT! TELL THEM I'M COMING OVER.
I'M SORRY, I HAVE TO CUT THIS SHORT! GET YOURSELF SORTED OUT AND I'LL SEE YOU AT THE TRACK. GOOD LUCK, SON!

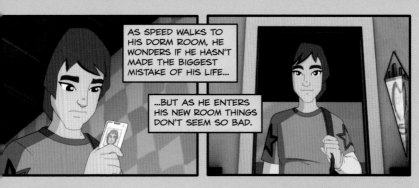

AS SPEED WALKS TO HIS DORM ROOM, HE WONDERS IF HE HASN'T MADE THE BIGGEST MISTAKE OF HIS LIFE...

...BUT AS HE ENTERS HIS NEW ROOM THINGS DON'T SEEM SO BAD.

THEN HE MEETS HIS NEW ROOMMATE.

YOU'RE THE NEW GUY RIGHT? I'M CONOR. WHAT'S YOUR NAME?

SPEED.

SPEED?! LIKE SPEED RACER?! NO WAY! THAT'S SO COOL!

I AM A HUGE SPEED FAN.

I MEAN A FAN OF THE SPEED RACER, NOT YOU. SO DON'T CREEP OUT.

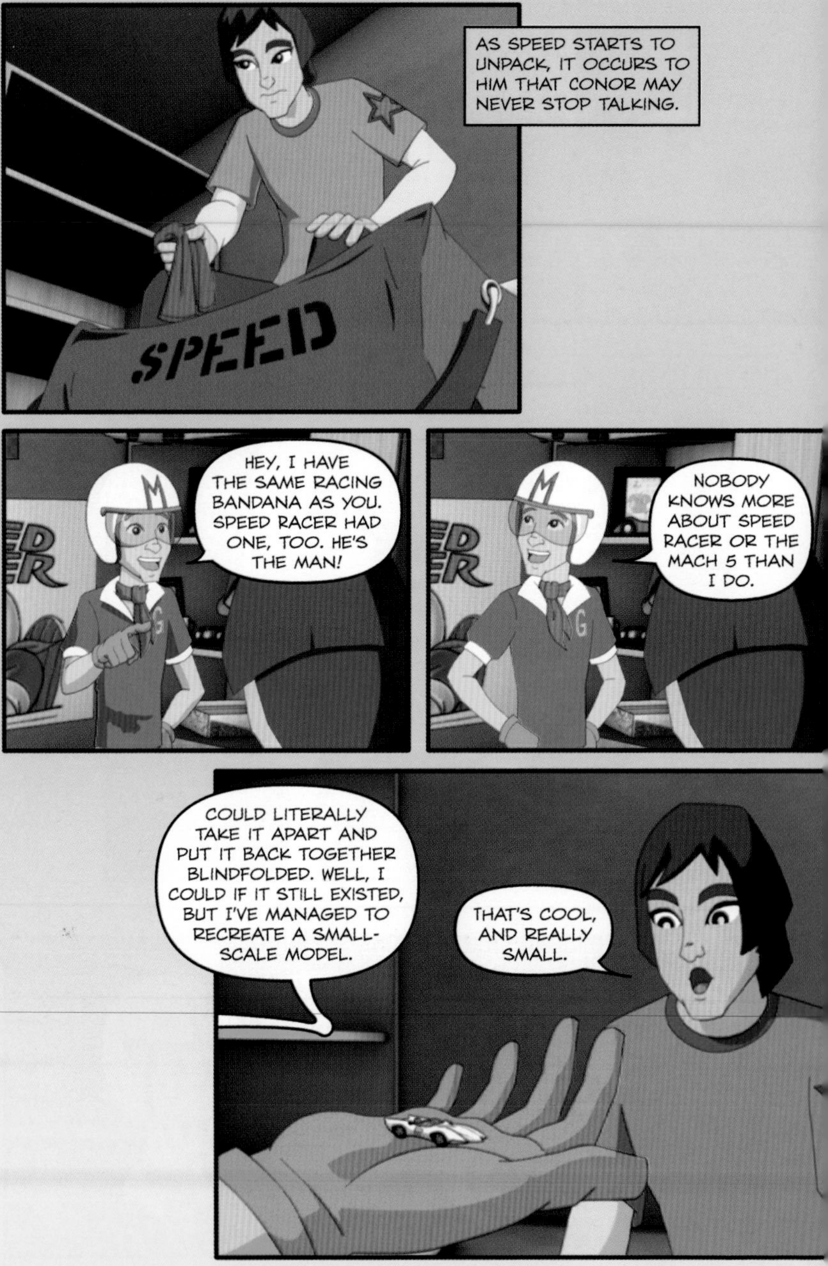
AS SPEED STARTS TO UNPACK, IT OCCURS TO HIM THAT CONOR MAY NEVER STOP TALKING.
SPEED
HEY, I HAVE THE SAME RACING BANDANA AS YOU. SPEED RACER HAD ONE, TOO. HE'S THE MAN!
NOBODY KNOWS MORE ABOUT SPEED RACER OR THE MACH 5 THAN I DO.
COULD LITERALLY TAKE IT APART AND PUT IT BACK TOGETHER BLINDFOLDED. WELL, I COULD IF IT STILL EXISTED, BUT I'VE MANAGED TO RECREATE A SMALL-SCALE MODEL.
THAT'S COOL, AND REALLY SMALL.

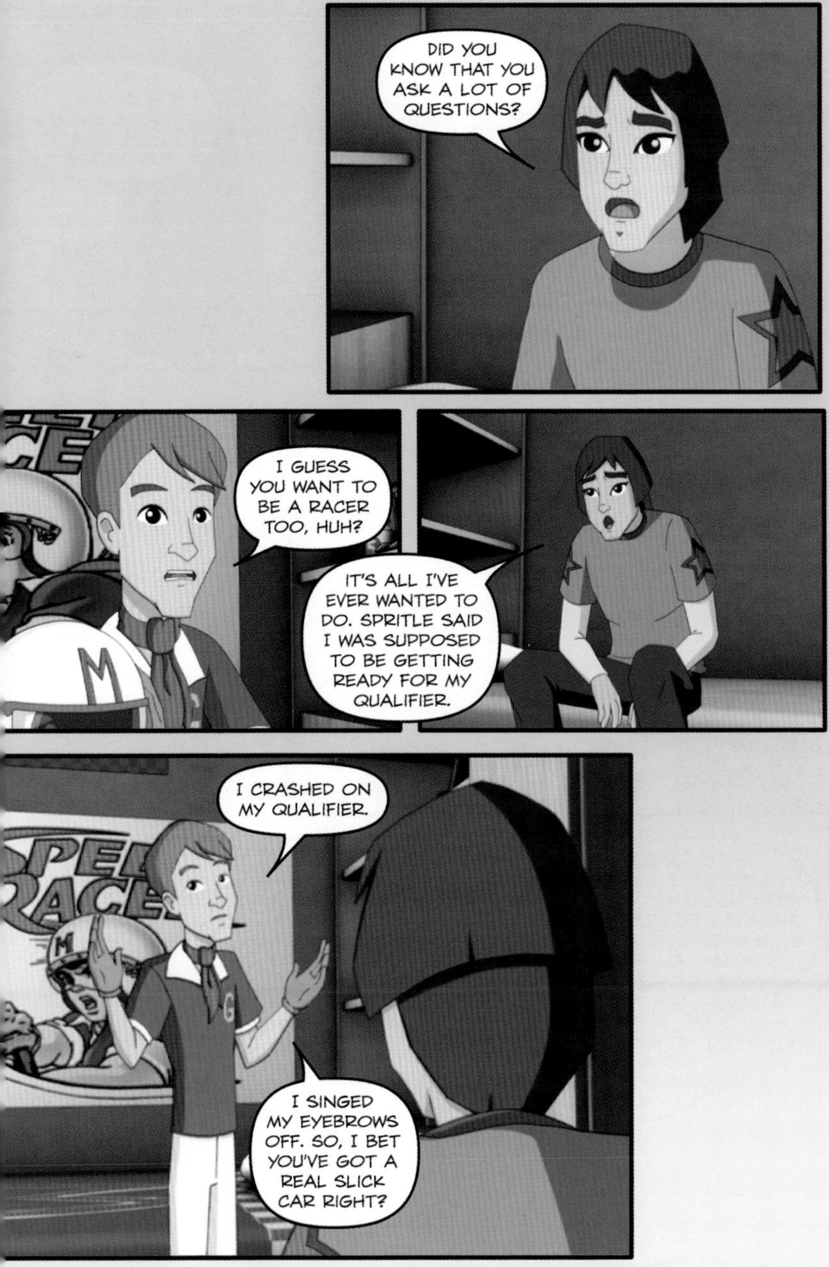
DID YOU KNOW THAT YOU ASK A LOT OF QUESTIONS?
I GUESS YOU WANT TO BE A RACER TOO, HUH?
IT'S ALL I'VE EVER WANTED TO DO. SPRITLE SAID I WAS SUPPOSED TO BE GETTING READY FOR MY QUALIFIER.
I CRASHED ON MY QUALIFIER.
I SINGED MY EYEBROWS OFF. SO, I BET YOU'VE GOT A REAL SLICK CAR RIGHT?

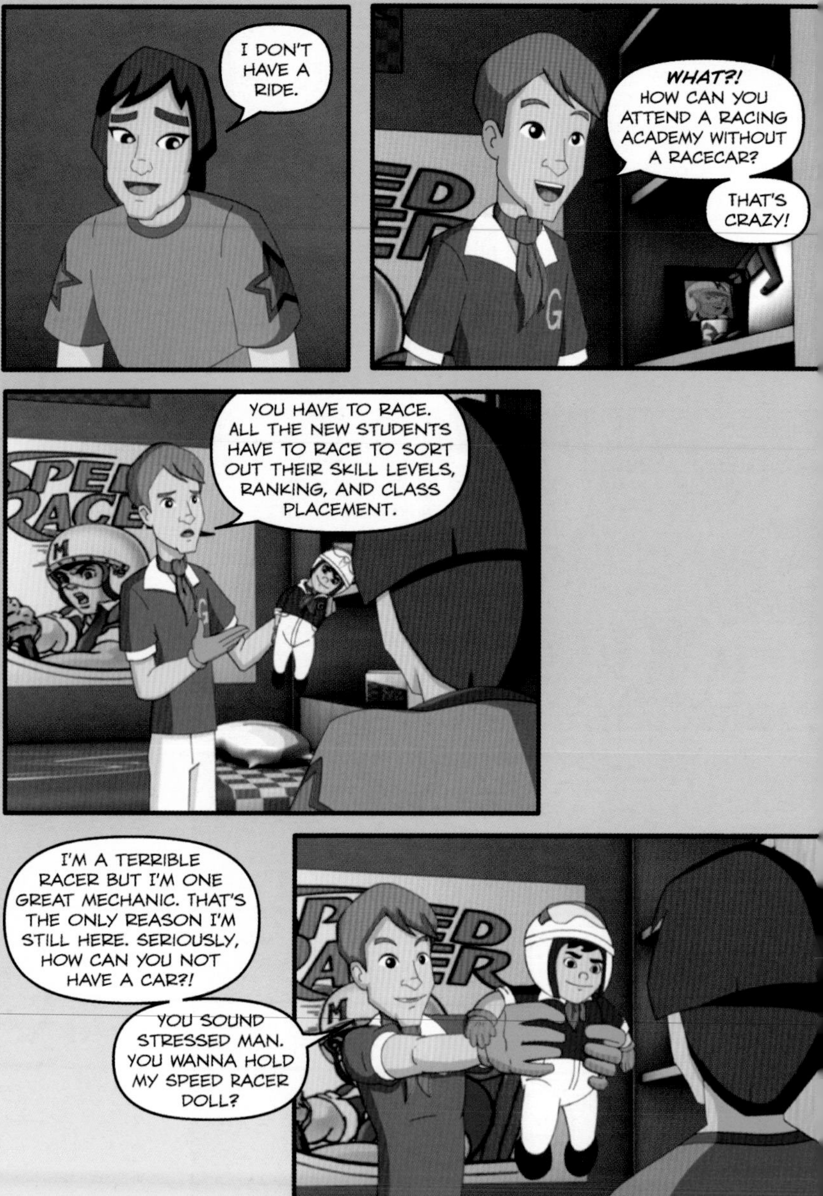
I DON'T HAVE A RIDE.
WHAT?! HOW CAN YOU ATTEND A RACING ACADEMY WITHOUT A RACECAR?
THAT'S CRAZY!
YOU HAVE TO RACE. ALL THE NEW STUDENTS HAVE TO RACE TO SORT OUT THEIR SKILL LEVELS, RANKING, AND CLASS PLACEMENT.
I'M A TERRIBLE RACER BUT I'M ONE GREAT MECHANIC. THAT'S THE ONLY REASON I'M STILL HERE. SERIOUSLY, HOW CAN YOU NOT HAVE A CAR?!
YOU SOUND STRESSED MAN. YOU WANNA HOLD MY SPEED RACER DOLL?

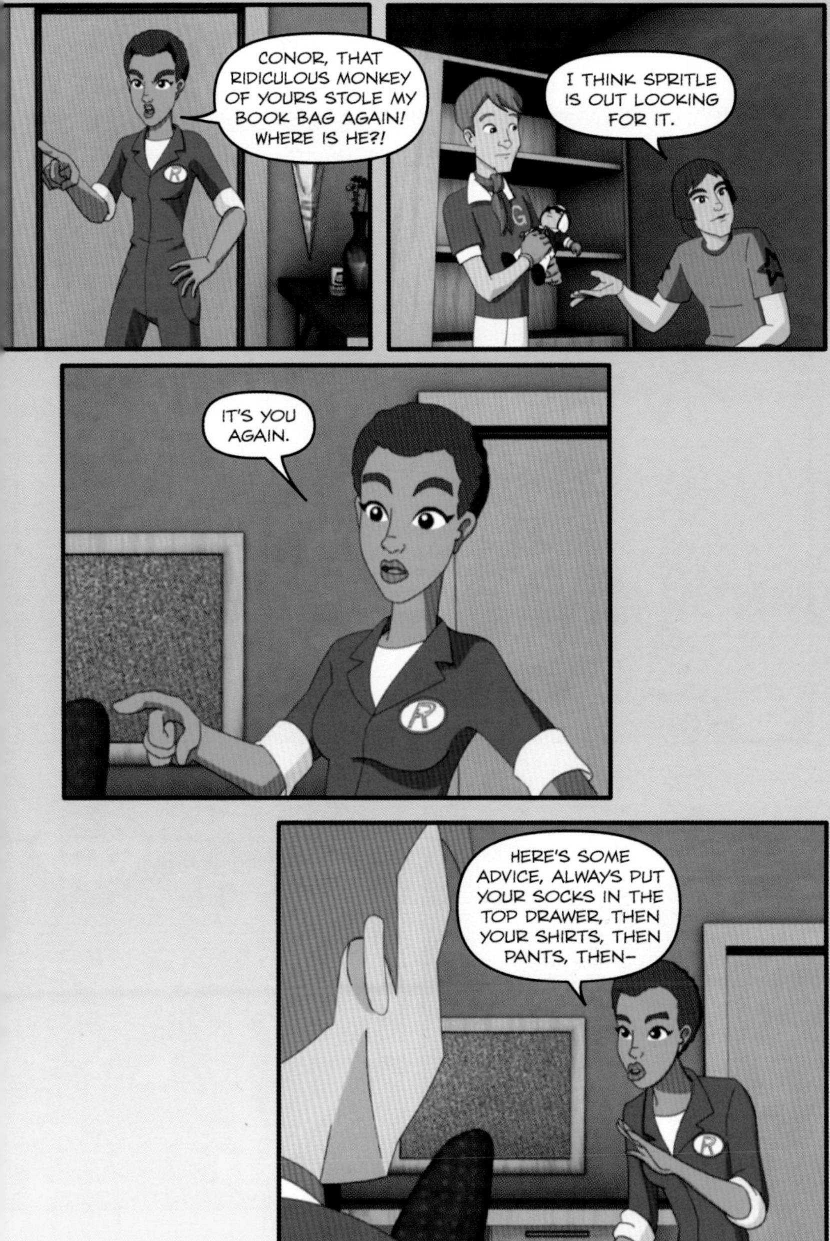
CONOR, THAT RIDICULOUS MONKEY OF YOURS STOLE MY BOOK BAG AGAIN! WHERE IS HE?!
I THINK SPRITLE IS OUT LOOKING FOR IT.
IT'S YOU AGAIN.
HERE'S SOME ADVICE, ALWAYS PUT YOUR SOCKS IN THE TOP DRAWER, THEN YOUR SHIRTS, THEN PANTS, THEN-

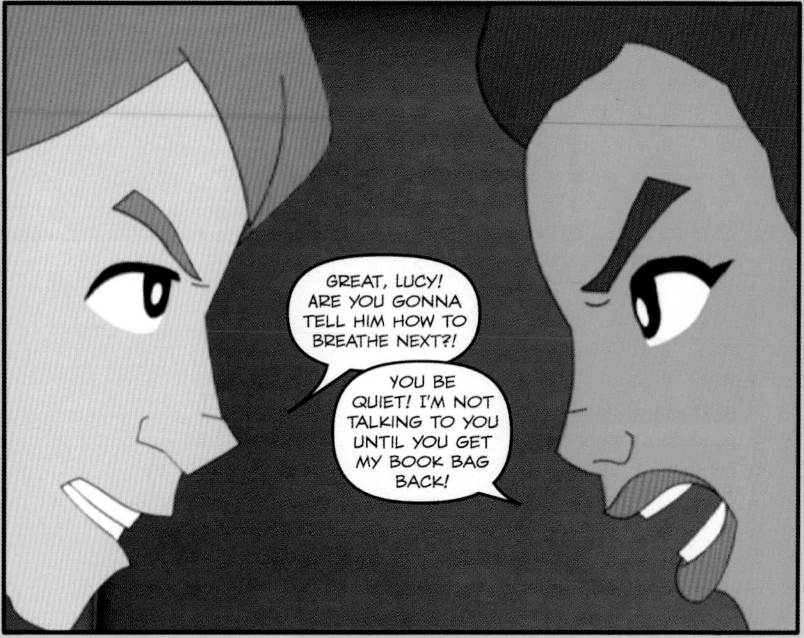
GREAT, LUCY! ARE YOU GONNA TELL HIM HOW TO BREATHE NEXT?!
YOU BE QUIET! I'M NOT TALKING TO YOU UNTIL YOU GET MY BOOK BAG BACK!

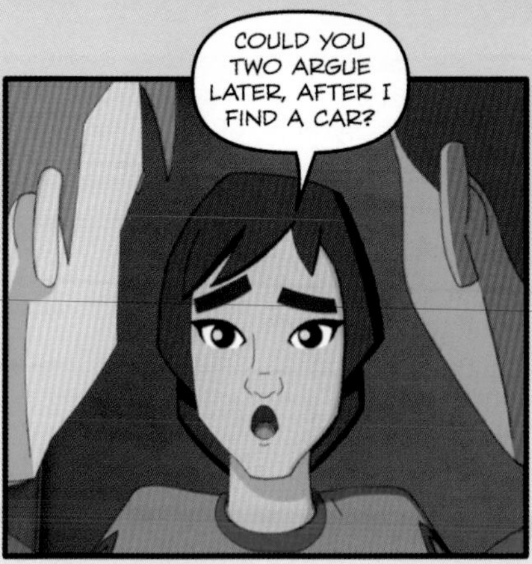
COULD YOU TWO ARGUE LATER, AFTER I FIND A CAR?

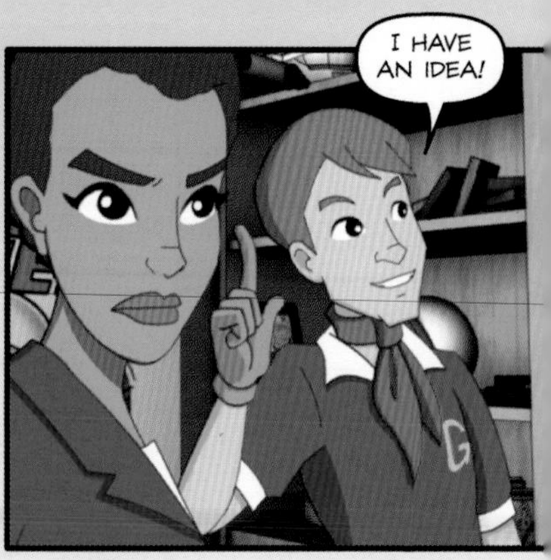
I HAVE AN IDEA!

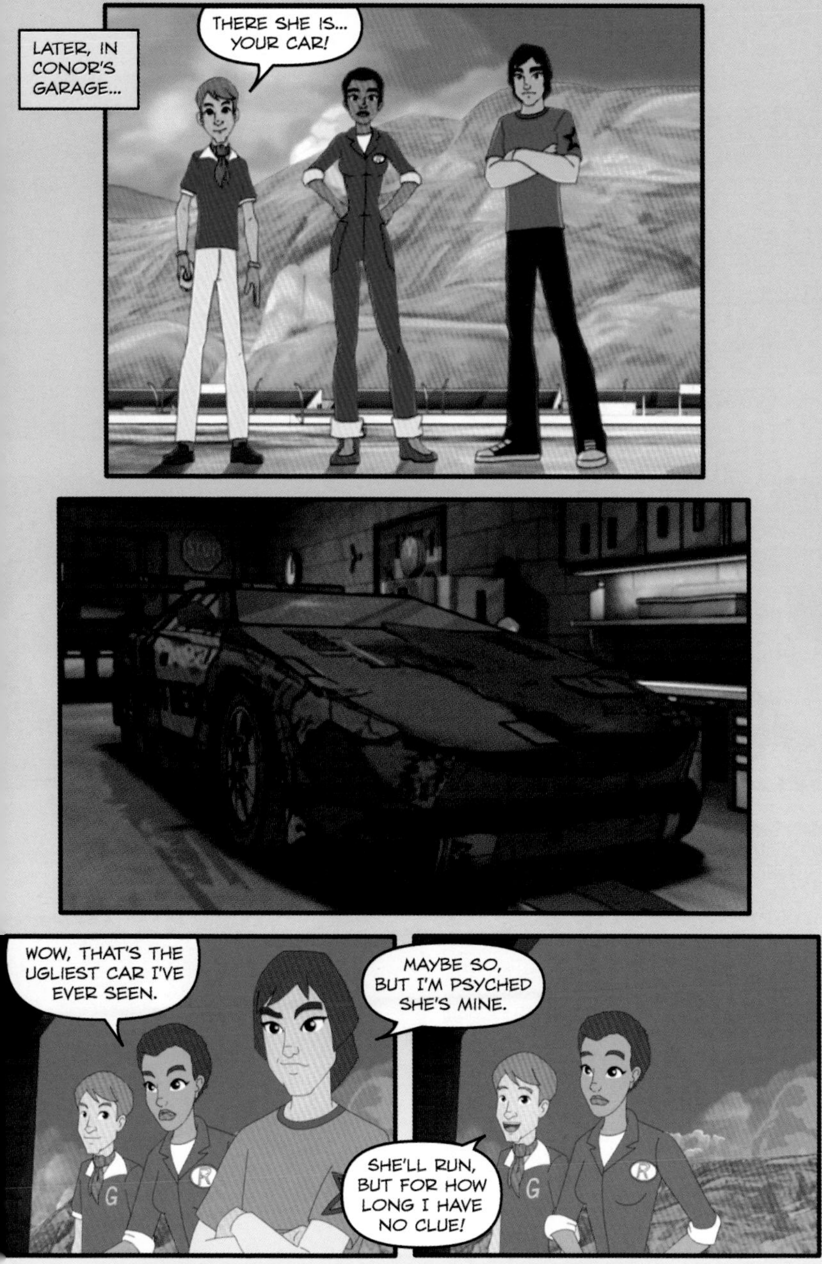
LATER, IN CONOR'S GARAGE...
THERE SHE IS... YOUR CAR!
WOW, THAT'S THE UGLIEST CAR I'VE EVER SEEN.
MAYBE SO, BUT I'M PSYCHED SHE'S MINE.
SHE'LL RUN, BUT FOR HOW LONG I HAVE NO CLUE!

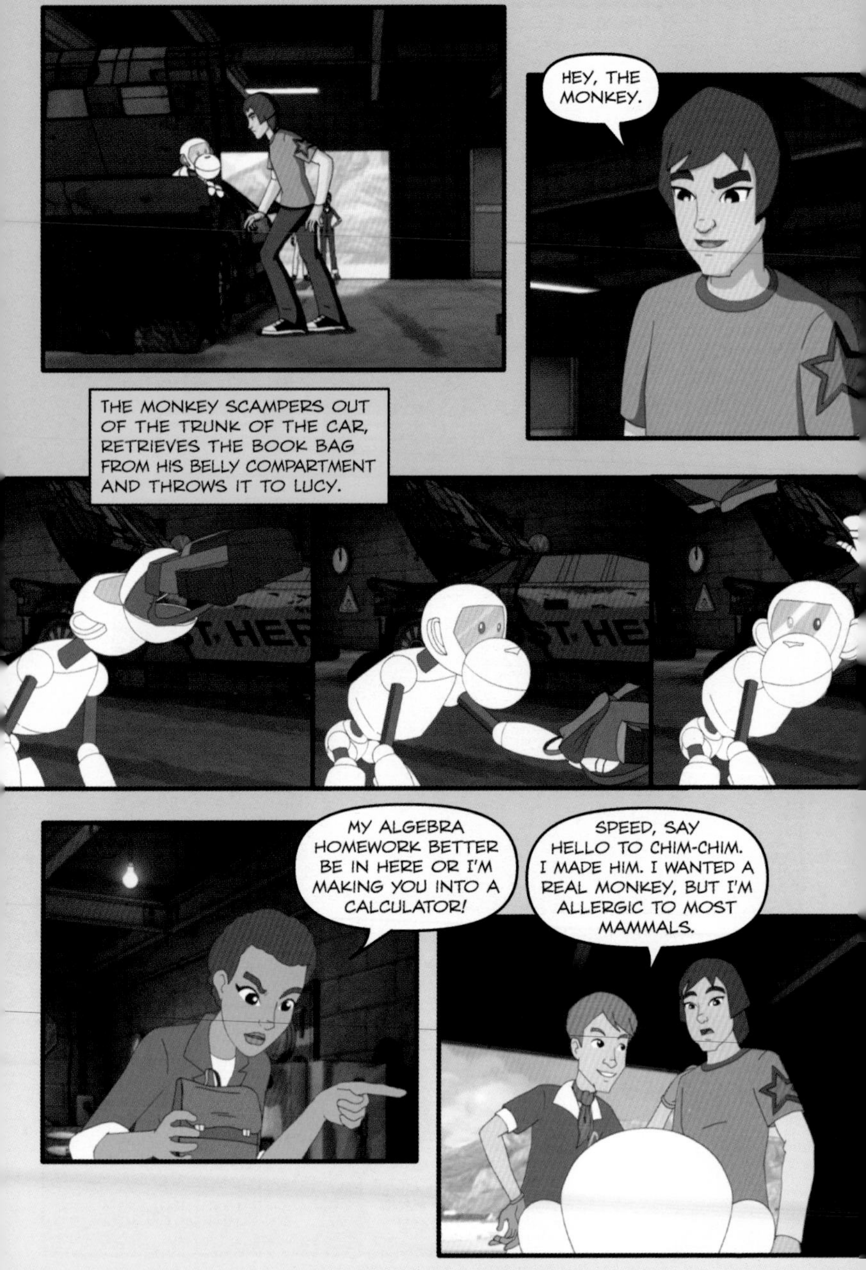
HEY, THE MONKEY.
THE MONKEY SCAMPERS OUT OF THE TRUNK OF THE CAR, RETRIEVES THE BOOK BAG FROM HIS BELLY COMPARTMENT AND THROWS IT TO LUCY.
MY ALGEBRA HOMEWORK BETTER BE IN HERE OR I'M MAKING YOU INTO A CALCULATOR!
SPEED, SAY HELLO TO CHIM-CHIM. I MADE HIM. I WANTED A REAL MONKEY, BUT I'M ALLERGIC TO MOST MAMMALS.

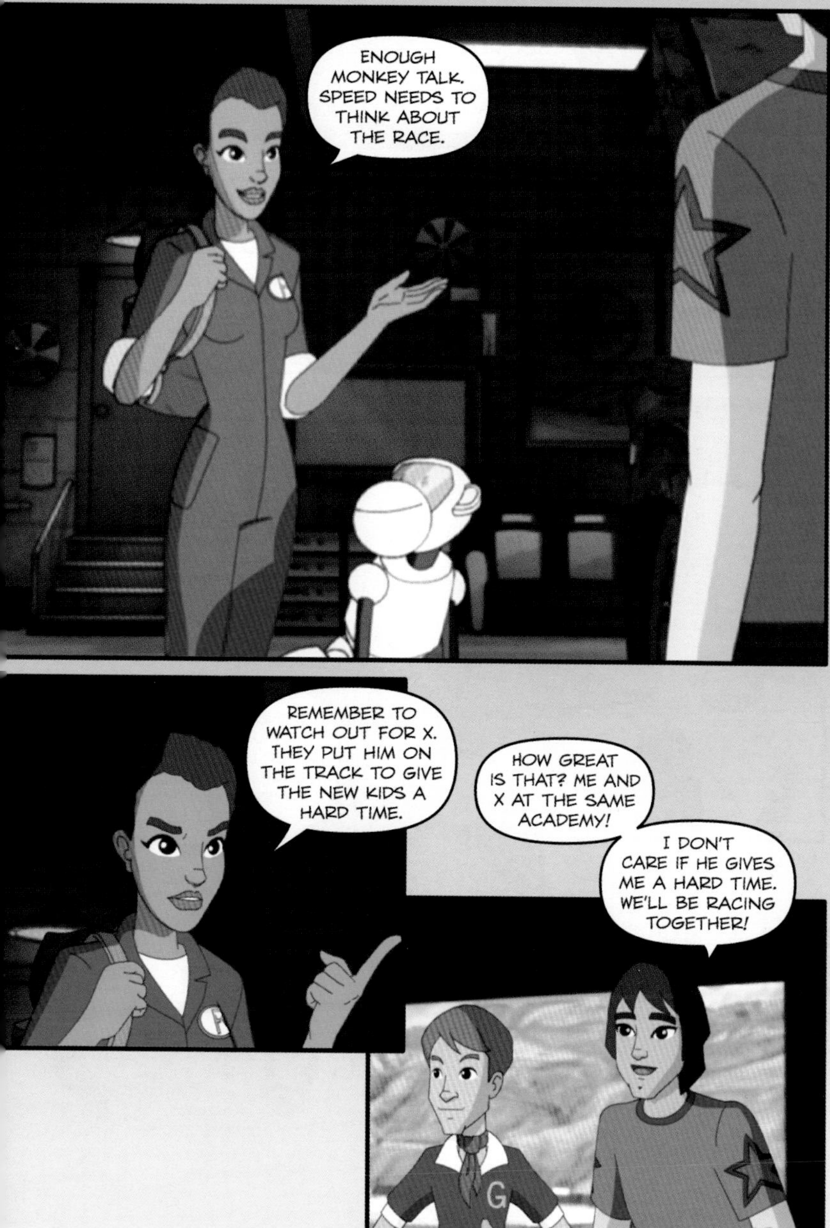
ENOUGH MONKEY TALK. SPEED NEEDS TO THINK ABOUT THE RACE.
REMEMBER TO WATCH OUT FOR X. THEY PUT HIM ON THE TRACK TO GIVE THE NEW KIDS A HARD TIME.
HOW GREAT IS THAT? ME AND X AT THE SAME ACADEMY!
I DON'T CARE IF HE GIVES ME A HARD TIME. WE'LL BE RACING TOGETHER!

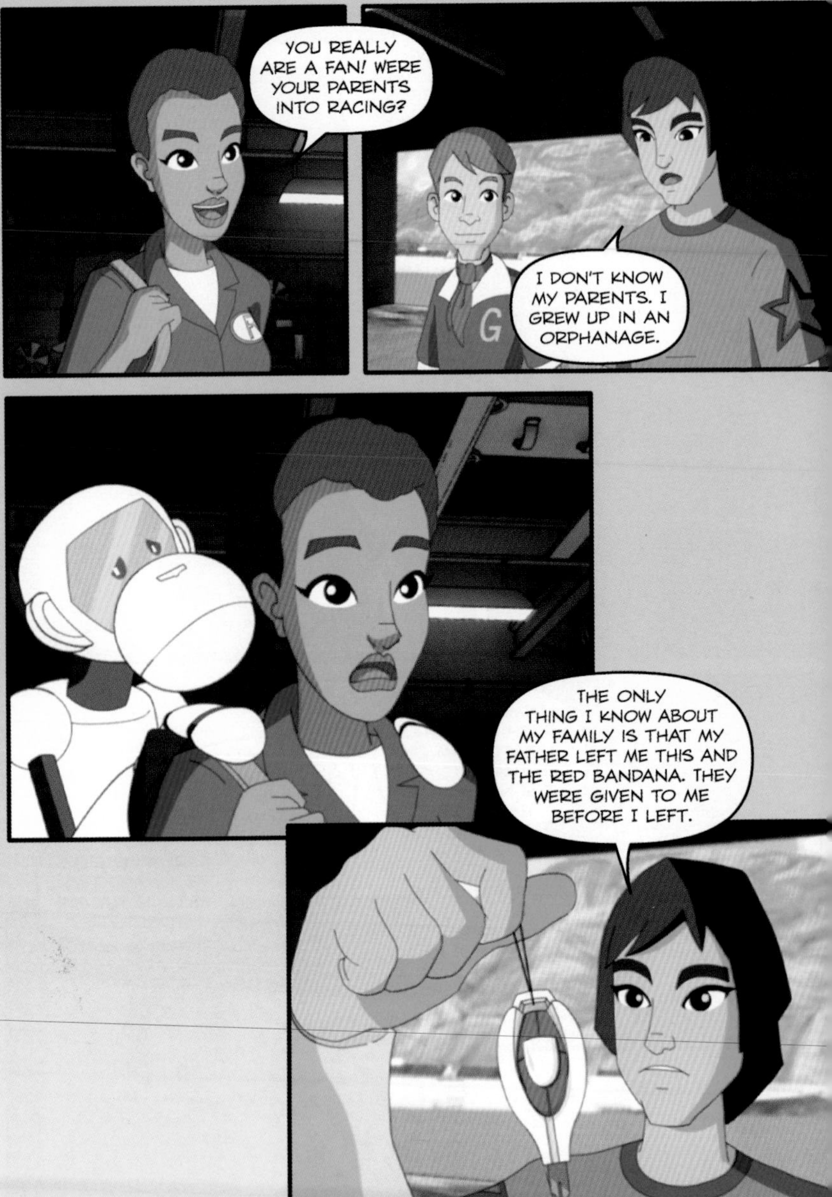
YOU REALLY ARE A FAN! WERE YOUR PARENTS INTO RACING?
I DON'T KNOW MY PARENTS. I GREW UP IN AN ORPHANAGE.
THE ONLY THING I KNOW ABOUT MY FAMILY IS THAT MY FATHER LEFT ME THIS AND THE RED BANDANA. THEY WERE GIVEN TO ME BEFORE I LEFT.

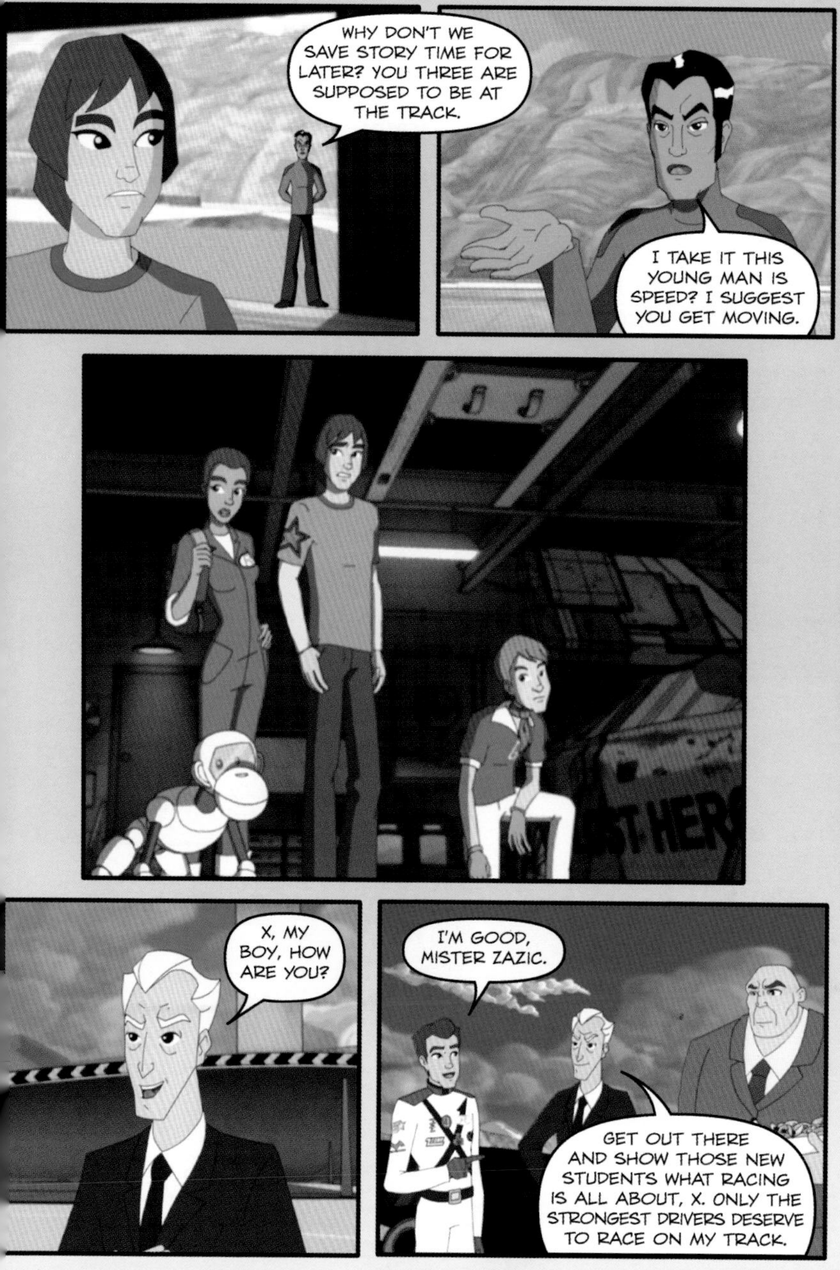
WHY DON'T WE SAVE STORY TIME FOR LATER? YOU THREE ARE SUPPOSED TO BE AT THE TRACK.
I TAKE IT THIS YOUNG MAN IS SPEED? I SUGGEST YOU GET MOVING.
X, MY BOY, HOW ARE YOU?
I'M GOOD, MISTER ZAZIC.
GET OUT THERE AND SHOW THOSE NEW STUDENTS WHAT RACING IS ALL ABOUT, X. ONLY THE STRONGEST DRIVERS DESERVE TO RACE ON MY TRACK.

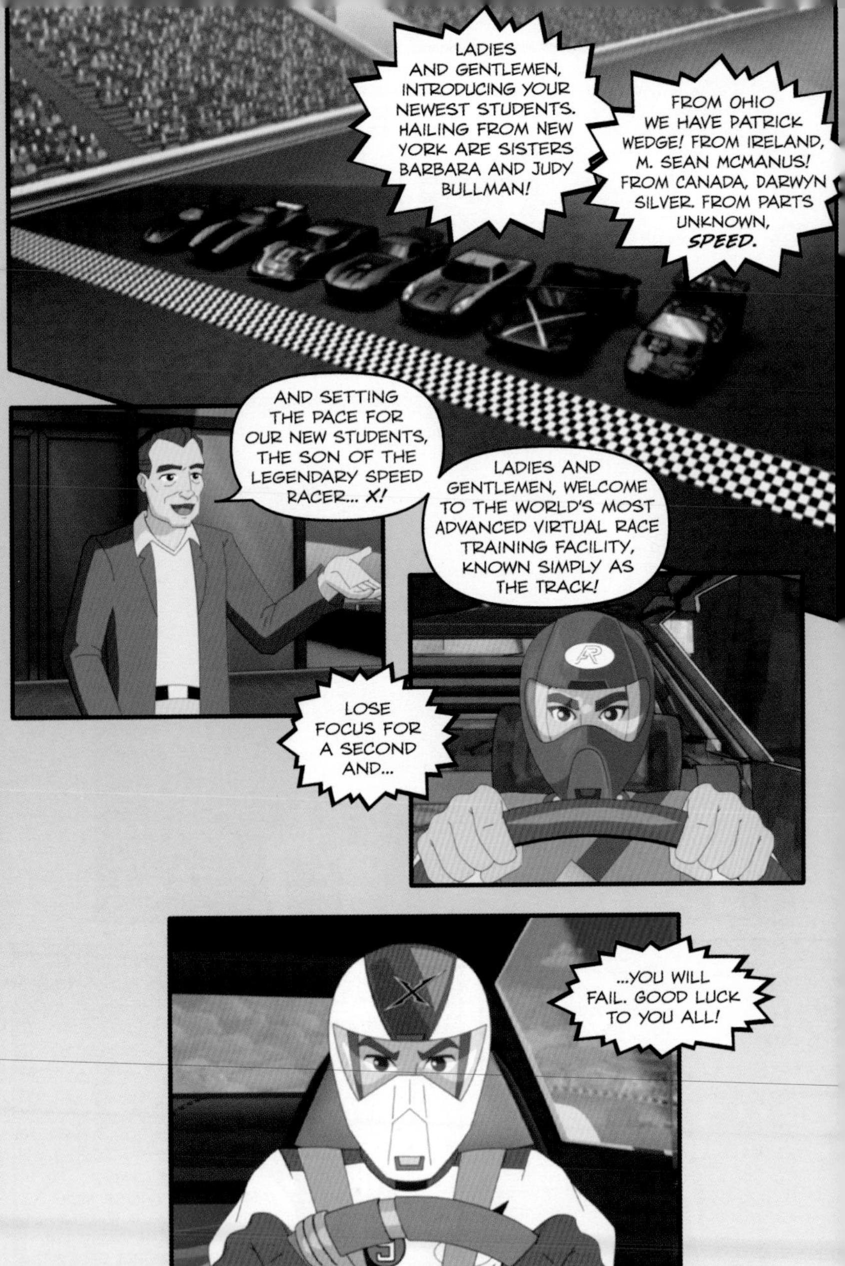
LADIES AND GENTLEMEN, INTRODUCING YOUR NEWEST STUDENTS. HAILING FROM NEW YORK ARE SISTERS BARBARA AND JUDY BULLMAN!
FROM OHIO WE HAVE PATRICK WEDGE! FROM IRELAND, M. SEAN MCMANUS! FROM CANADA, DARWYN SILVER. FROM PARTS UNKNOWN, SPEED.
AND SETTING THE PACE FOR OUR NEW STUDENTS, THE SON OF THE LEGENDARY SPEED RACER... X!
LADIES AND GENTLEMEN, WELCOME TO THE WORLD'S MOST ADVANCED VIRTUAL RACE TRAINING FACILITY, KNOWN SIMPLY AS THE TRACK!
LOSE FOCUS FOR A SECOND AND...
...YOU WILL FAIL. GOOD LUCK TO YOU ALL!

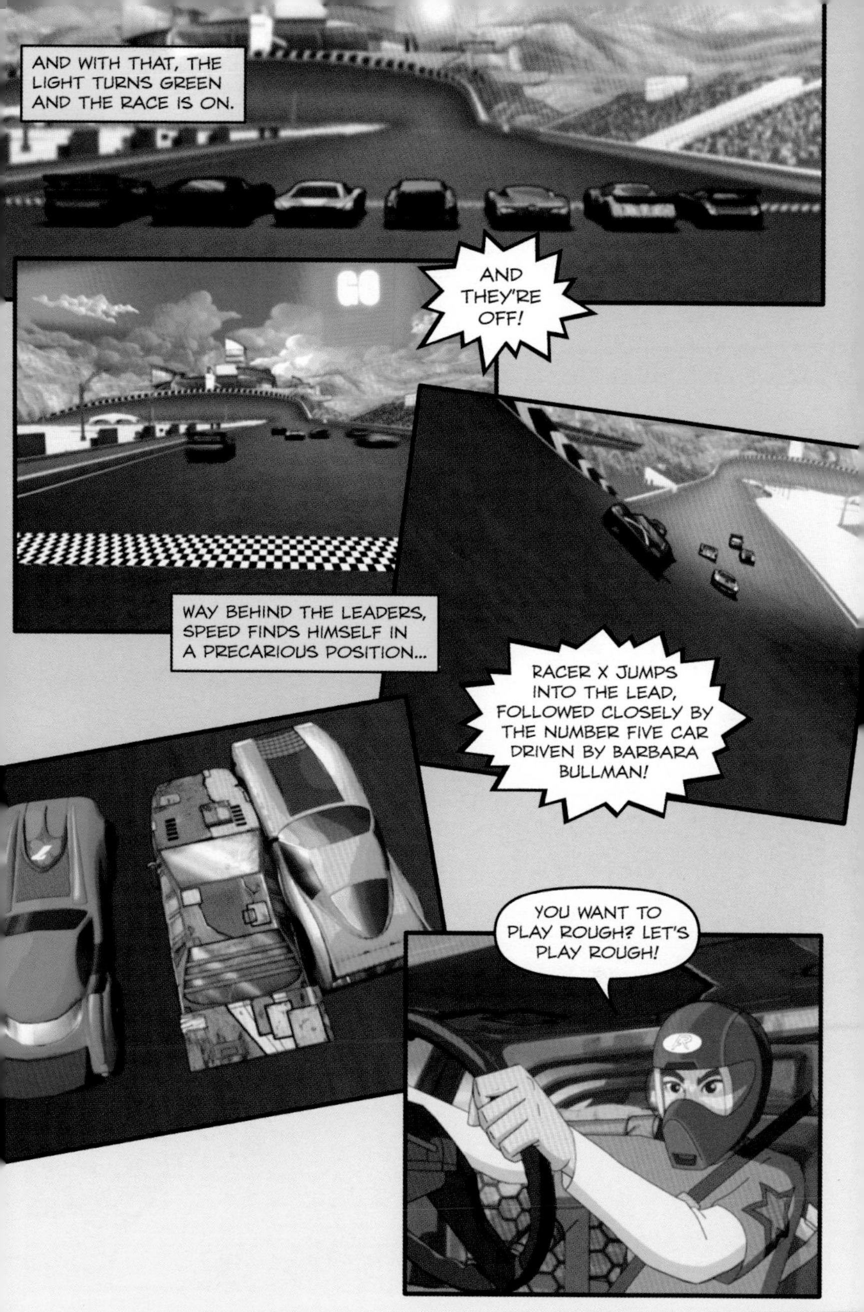
AND WITH THAT, THE LIGHT TURNS GREEN AND THE RACE IS ON.
GO
AND THEY'RE OFF!
WAY BEHIND THE LEADERS, SPEED FINDS HIMSELF IN A PRECARIOUS POSITION...
RACER X JUMPS INTO THE LEAD, FOLLOWED CLOSELY BY THE NUMBER FIVE CAR DRIVEN BY BARBARA BULLMAN!
YOU WANT TO PLAY ROUGH? LET'S PLAY ROUGH!

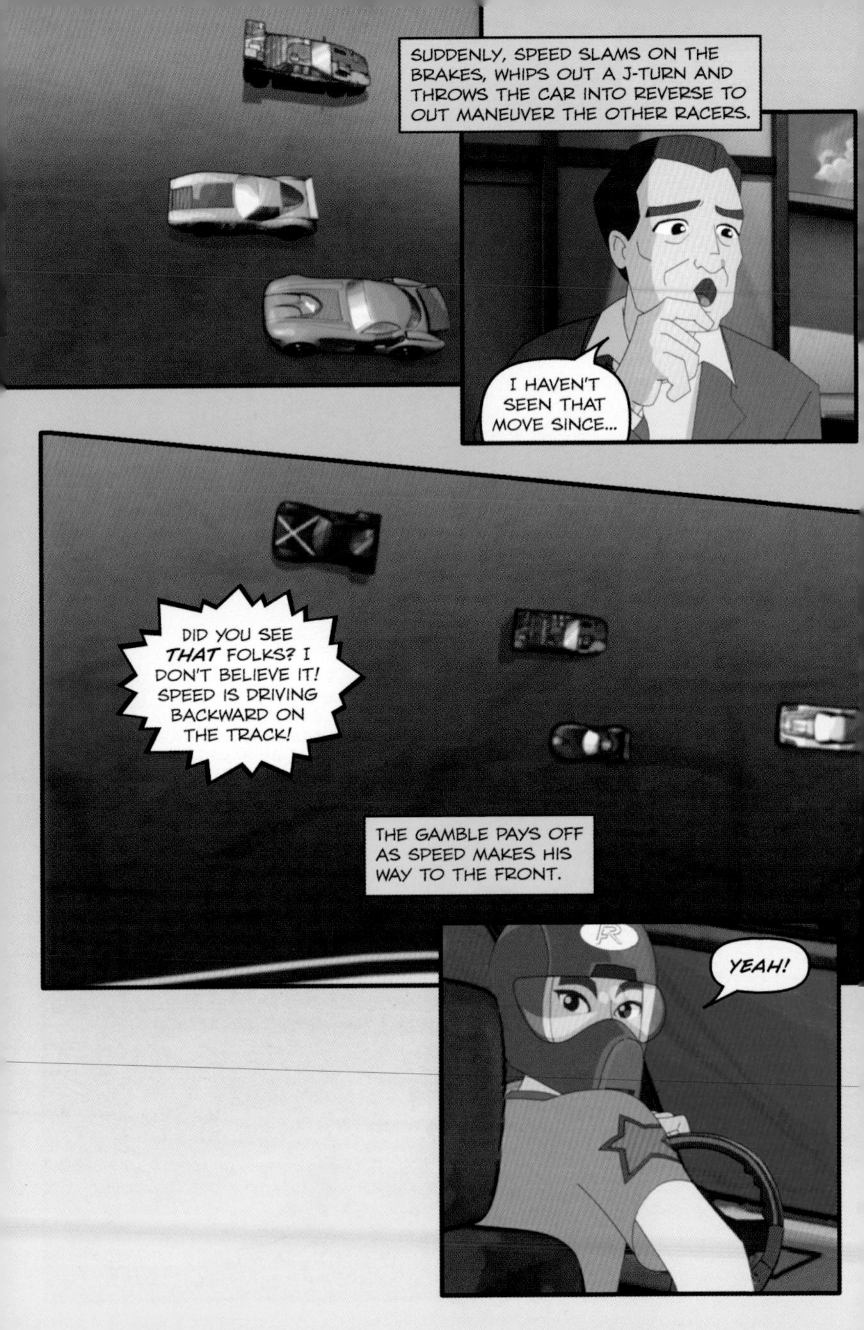
SUDDENLY, SPEED SLAMS ON THE BRAKES, WHIPS OUT A J-TURN AND THROWS THE CAR INTO REVERSE TO OUT MANEUVER THE OTHER RACERS.
I HAVEN'T SEEN THAT MOVE SINCE...
DID YOU SEE *THAT* FOLKS? I DON'T BELIEVE IT! SPEED IS DRIVING BACKWARD ON THE TRACK!
THE GAMBLE PAYS OFF AS SPEED MAKES HIS WAY TO THE FRONT.
YEAH!

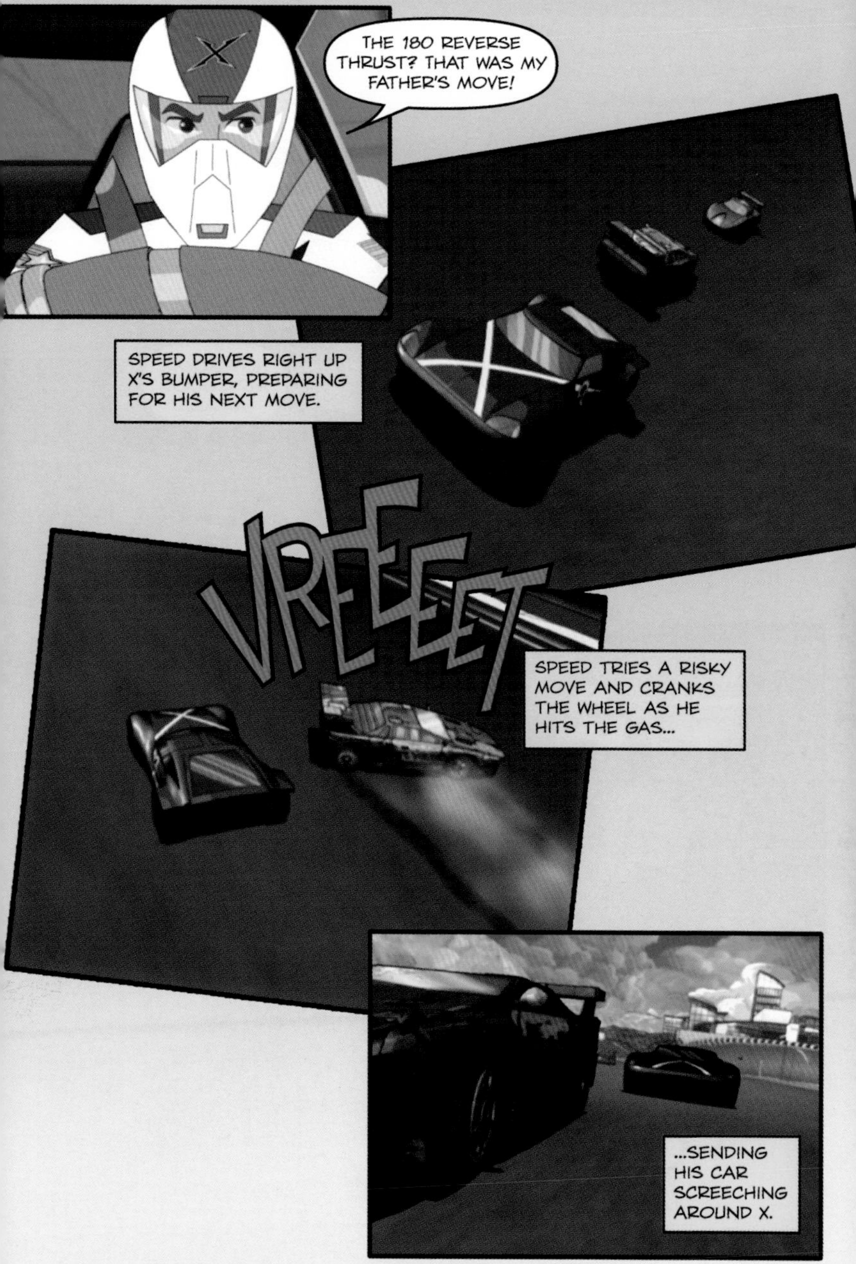
THE 180 REVERSE THRUST? THAT WAS MY FATHER'S MOVE!
SPEED DRIVES RIGHT UP X'S BUMPER, PREPARING FOR HIS NEXT MOVE.
VREEEEET
SPEED TRIES A RISKY MOVE AND CRANKS THE WHEEL AS HE HITS THE GAS...
...SENDING HIS CAR SCREECHING AROUND X.

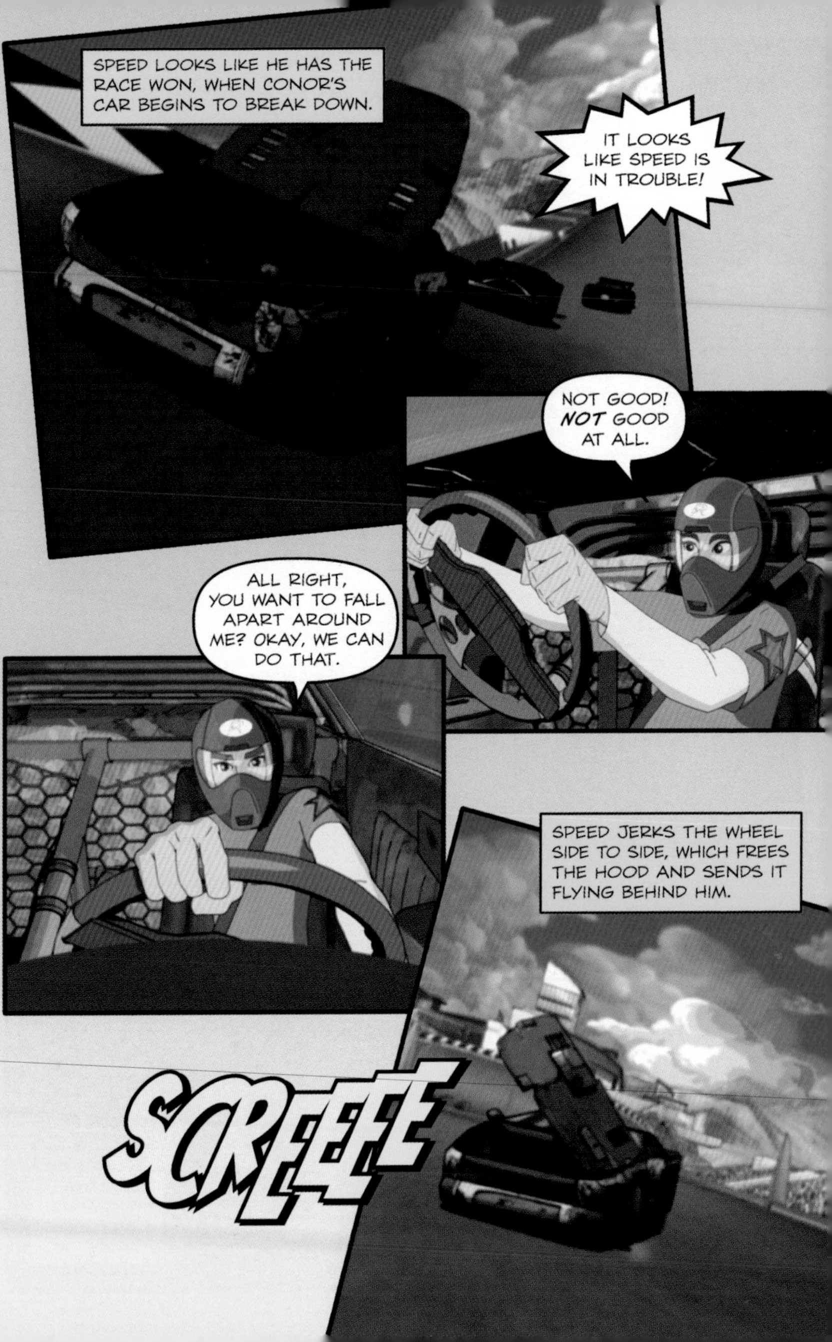
SPEED LOOKS LIKE HE HAS THE RACE WON, WHEN CONOR'S CAR BEGINS TO BREAK DOWN.
IT LOOKS LIKE SPEED IS IN TROUBLE!
NOT GOOD! NOT GOOD AT ALL.
ALL RIGHT, YOU WANT TO FALL APART AROUND ME? OKAY, WE CAN DO THAT.
SPEED JERKS THE WHEEL SIDE TO SIDE, WHICH FREES THE HOOD AND SENDS IT FLYING BEHIND HIM.
SCREEEE

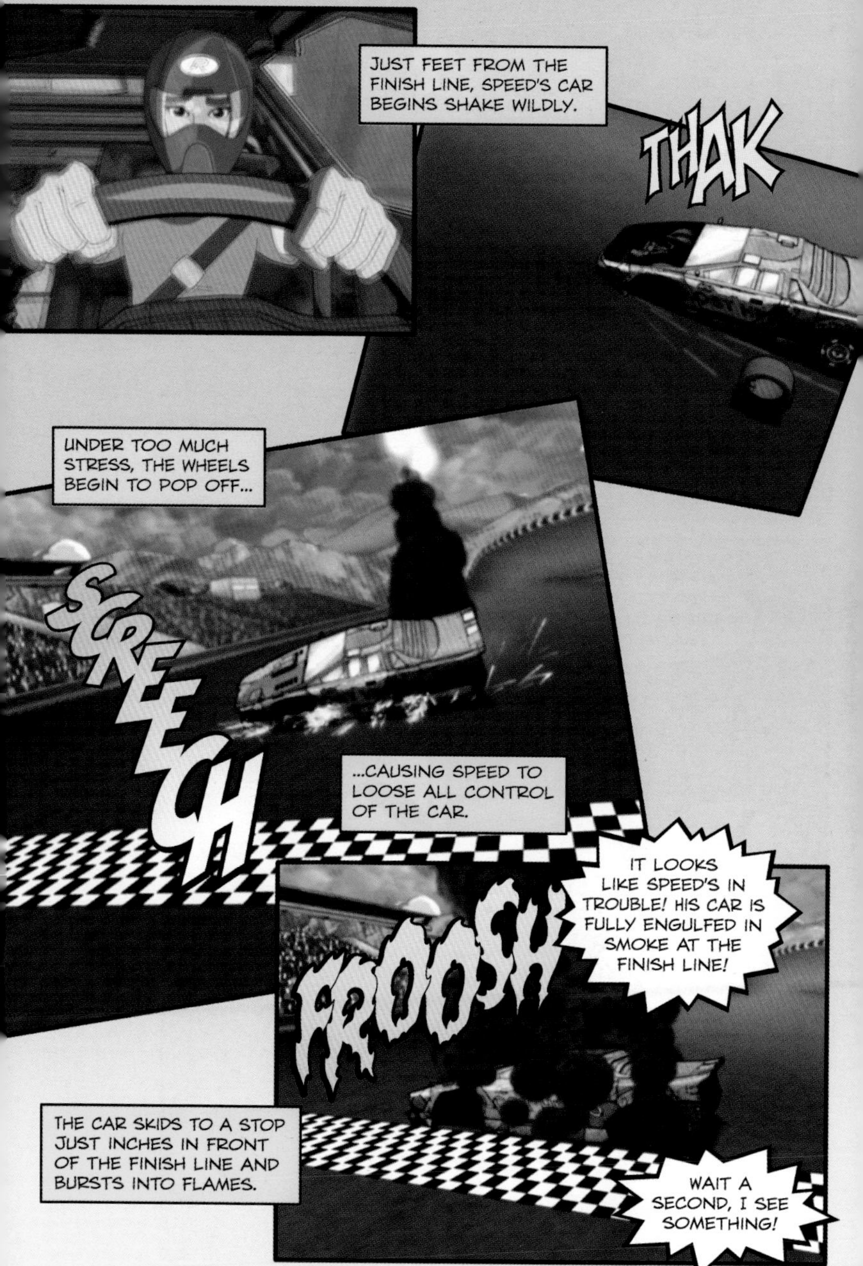
JUST FEET FROM THE FINISH LINE, SPEED'S CAR BEGINS SHAKE WILDLY.
THAK
UNDER TOO MUCH STRESS, THE WHEELS BEGIN TO POP OFF...
SCREEECH
...CAUSING SPEED TO LOOSE ALL CONTROL OF THE CAR.
FROOSH
IT LOOKS LIKE SPEED'S IN TROUBLE! HIS CAR IS FULLY ENGULFED IN SMOKE AT THE FINISH LINE!
THE CAR SKIDS TO A STOP JUST INCHES IN FRONT OF THE FINISH LINE AND BURSTS INTO FLAMES.
WAIT A SECOND, I SEE SOMETHING!

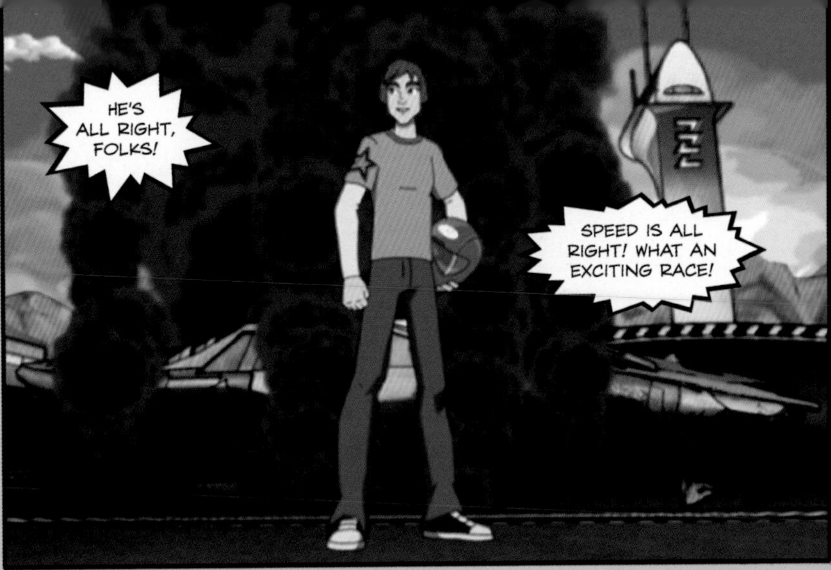
HE'S ALL RIGHT, FOLKS!
SPEED IS ALL RIGHT! WHAT AN EXCITING RACE!

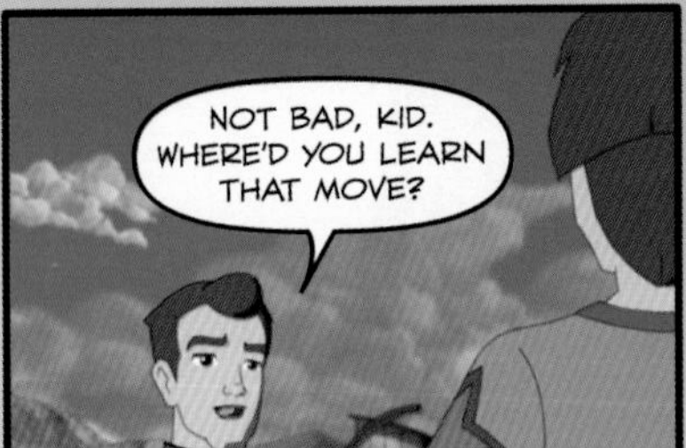
NOT BAD, KID. WHERE'D YOU LEARN THAT MOVE?

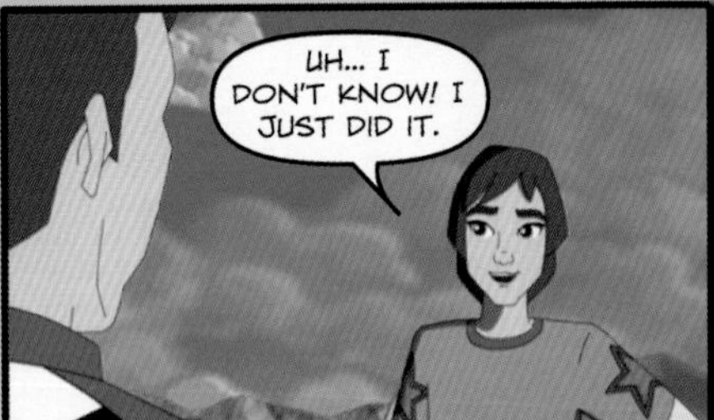
UH... I DON'T KNOW! I JUST DID IT.

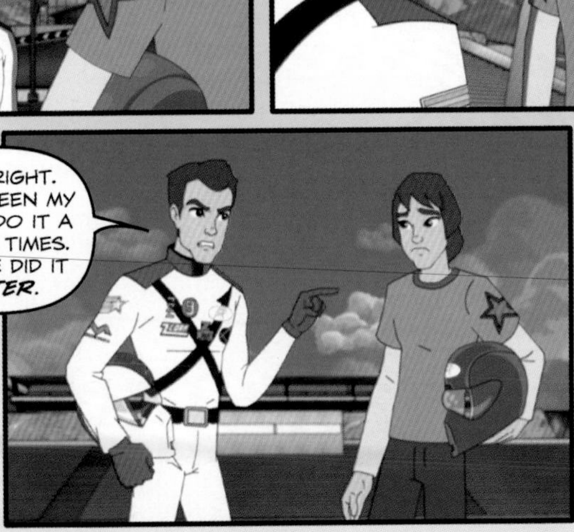
YEAH, RIGHT. YOU'VE SEEN MY FATHER DO IT A MILLION TIMES. ONLY HE DID IT *BETTER*.

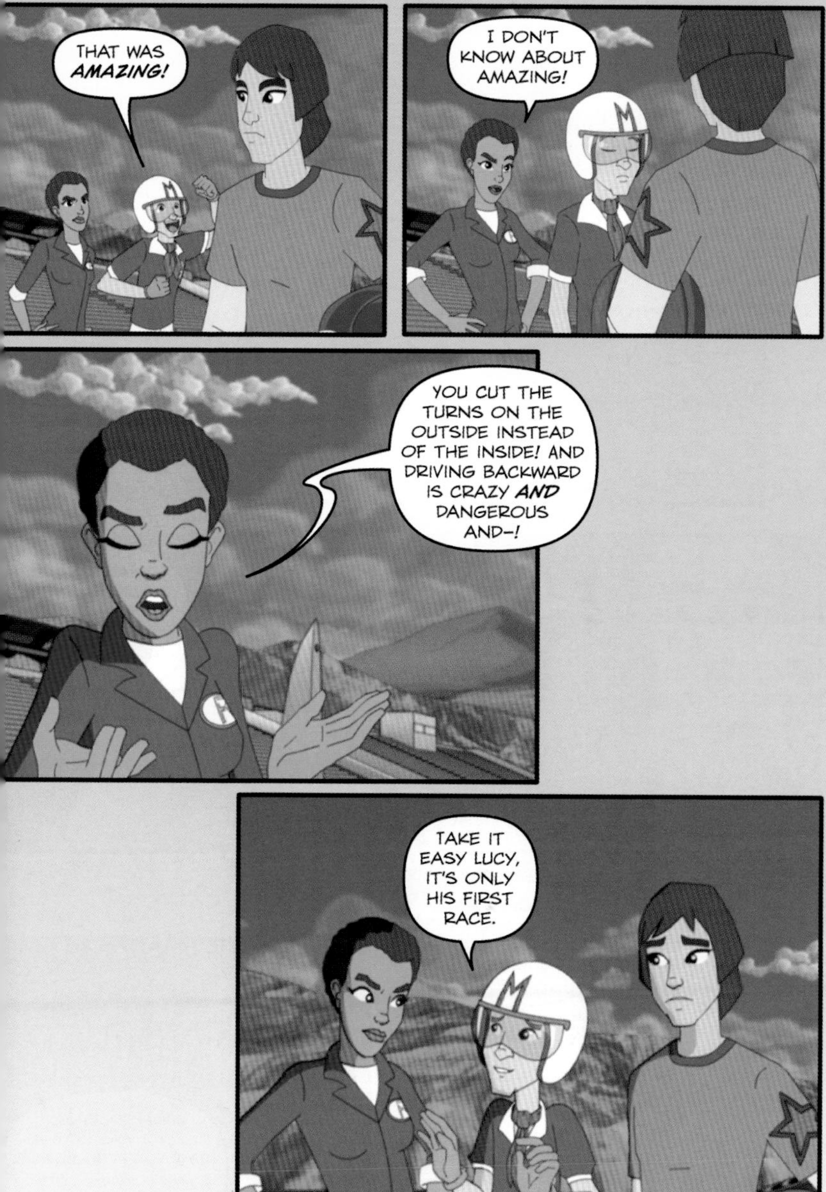
THAT WAS AMAZING!
I DON'T KNOW ABOUT AMAZING!
YOU CUT THE TURNS ON THE OUTSIDE INSTEAD OF THE INSIDE! AND DRIVING BACKWARD IS CRAZY AND DANGEROUS AND--!
TAKE IT EASY LUCY, IT'S ONLY HIS FIRST RACE.

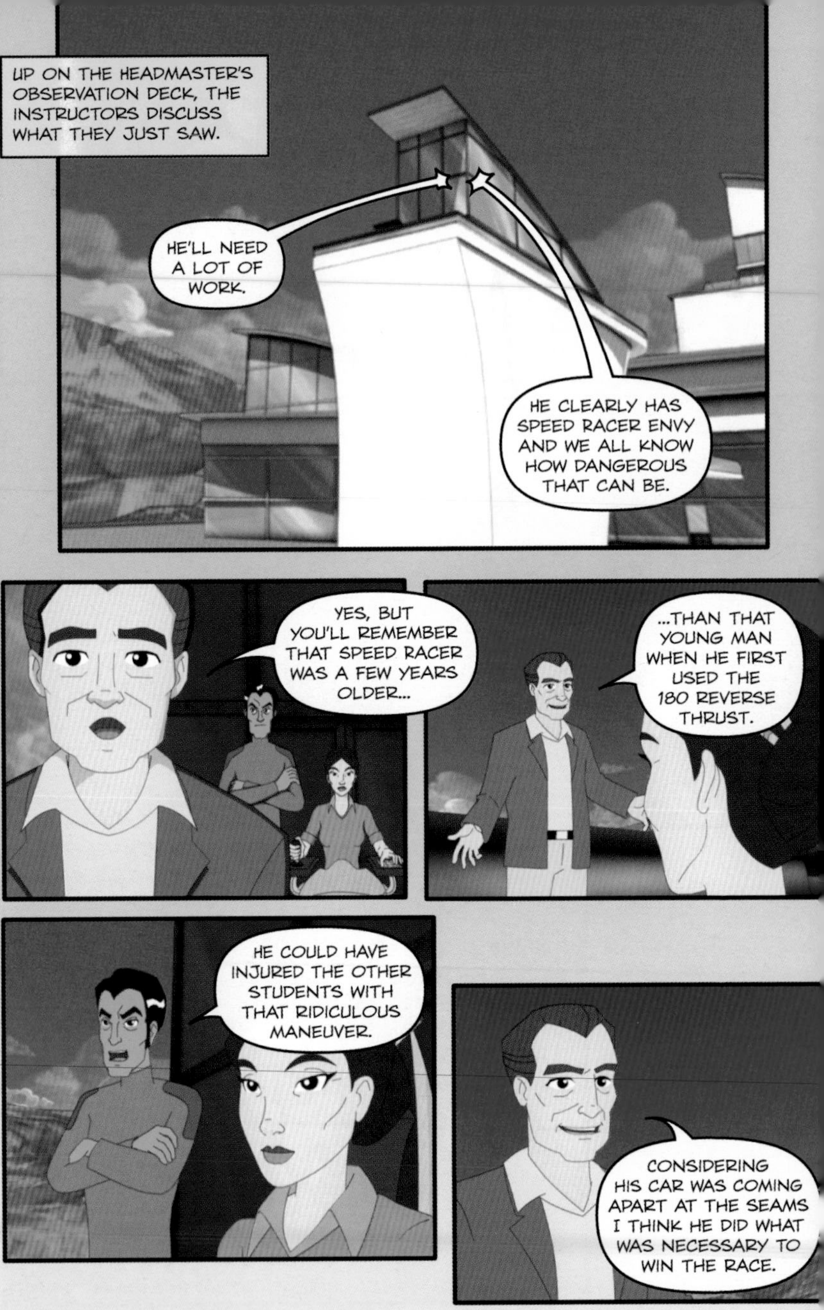
UP ON THE HEADMASTER'S OBSERVATION DECK, THE INSTRUCTORS DISCUSS WHAT THEY JUST SAW.
HE'LL NEED A LOT OF WORK.
HE CLEARLY HAS SPEED RACER ENVY AND WE ALL KNOW HOW DANGEROUS THAT CAN BE.
YES, BUT YOU'LL REMEMBER THAT SPEED RACER WAS A FEW YEARS OLDER...
...THAN THAT YOUNG MAN WHEN HE FIRST USED THE 180 REVERSE THRUST.
HE COULD HAVE INJURED THE OTHER STUDENTS WITH THAT RIDICULOUS MANEUVER.
CONSIDERING HIS CAR WAS COMING APART AT THE SEAMS I THINK HE DID WHAT WAS NECESSARY TO WIN THE RACE.

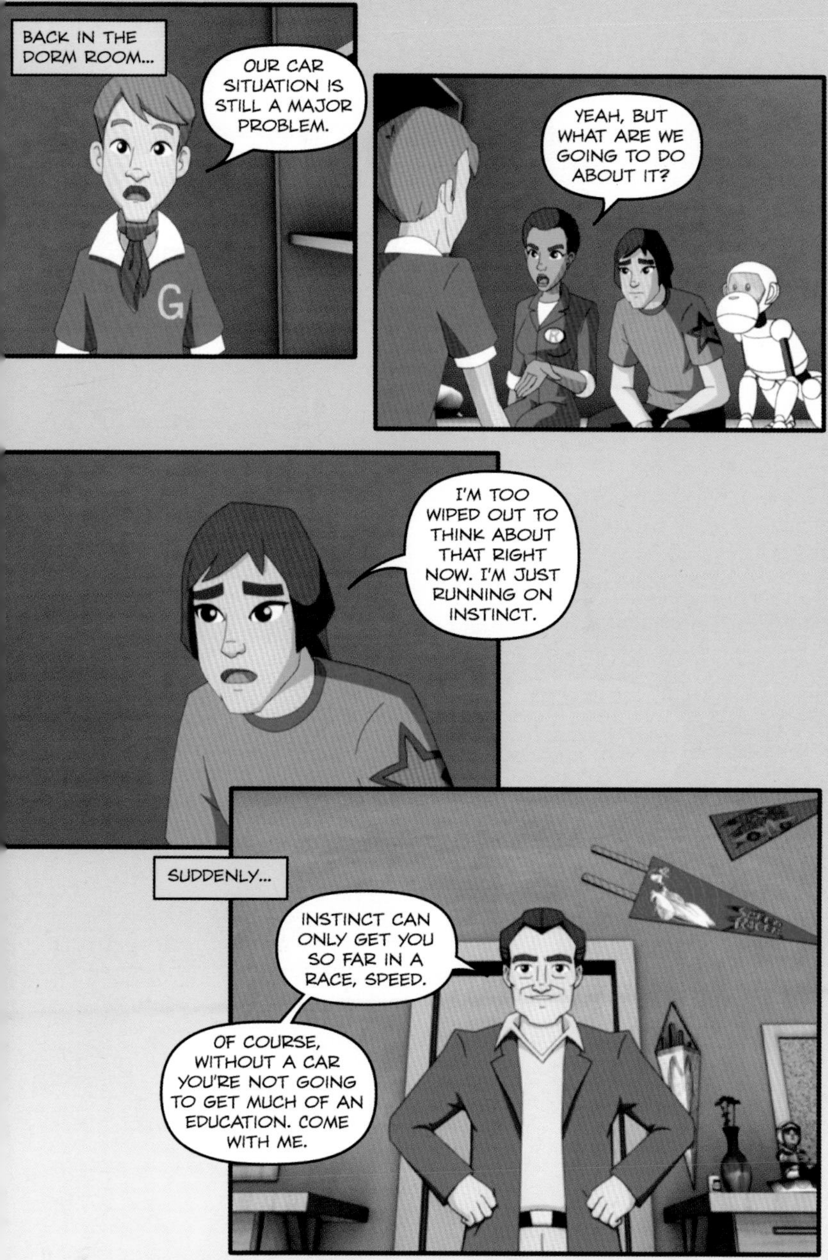
BACK IN THE DORM ROOM...
OUR CAR SITUATION IS STILL A MAJOR PROBLEM.
YEAH, BUT WHAT ARE WE GOING TO DO ABOUT IT?
I'M TOO WIPED OUT TO THINK ABOUT THAT RIGHT NOW. I'M JUST RUNNING ON INSTINCT.
SUDDENLY...
INSTINCT CAN ONLY GET YOU SO FAR IN A RACE, SPEED.
OF COURSE, WITHOUT A CAR YOU'RE NOT GOING TO GET MUCH OF AN EDUCATION. COME WITH ME.

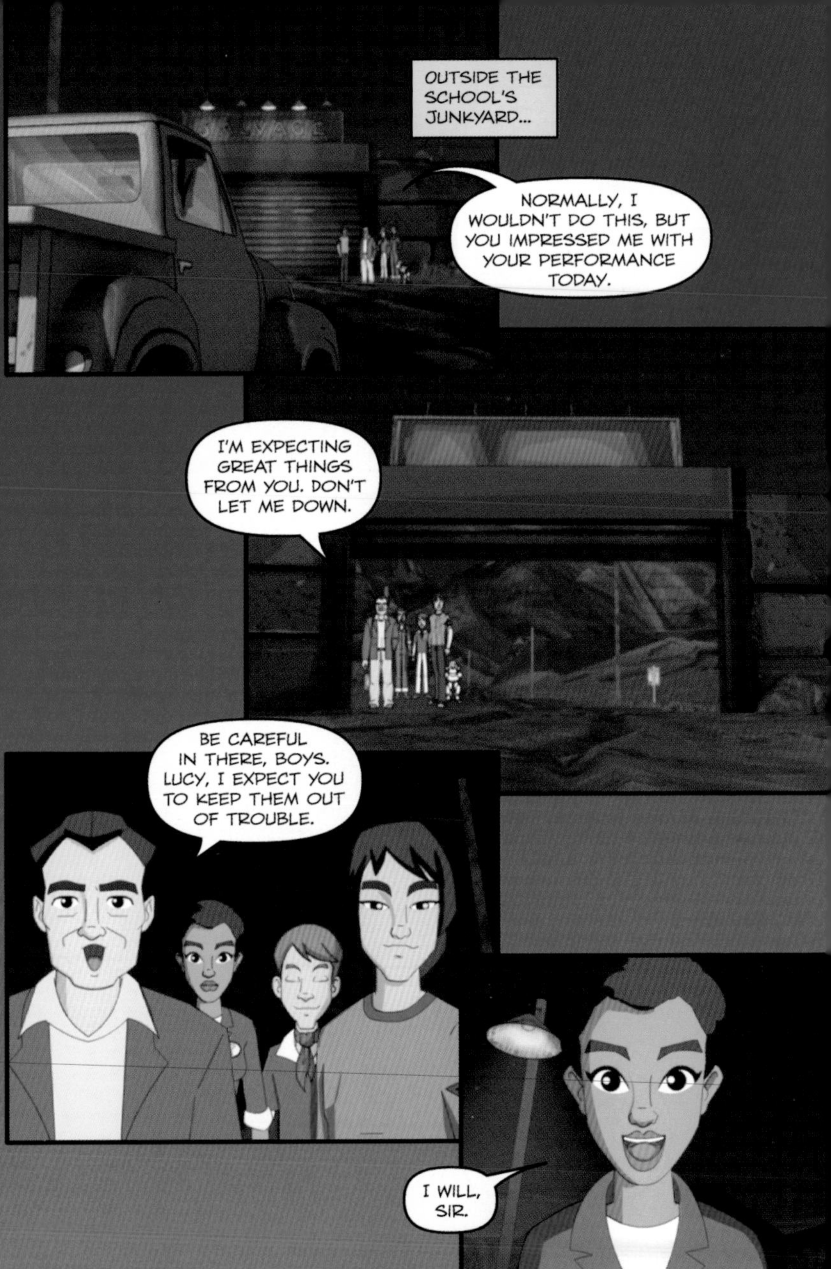
OUTSIDE THE SCHOOL'S JUNKYARD...
NORMALLY, I WOULDN'T DO THIS, BUT YOU IMPRESSED ME WITH YOUR PERFORMANCE TODAY.
I'M EXPECTING GREAT THINGS FROM YOU. DON'T LET ME DOWN.
BE CAREFUL IN THERE, BOYS. LUCY, I EXPECT YOU TO KEEP THEM OUT OF TROUBLE.
I WILL, SIR.

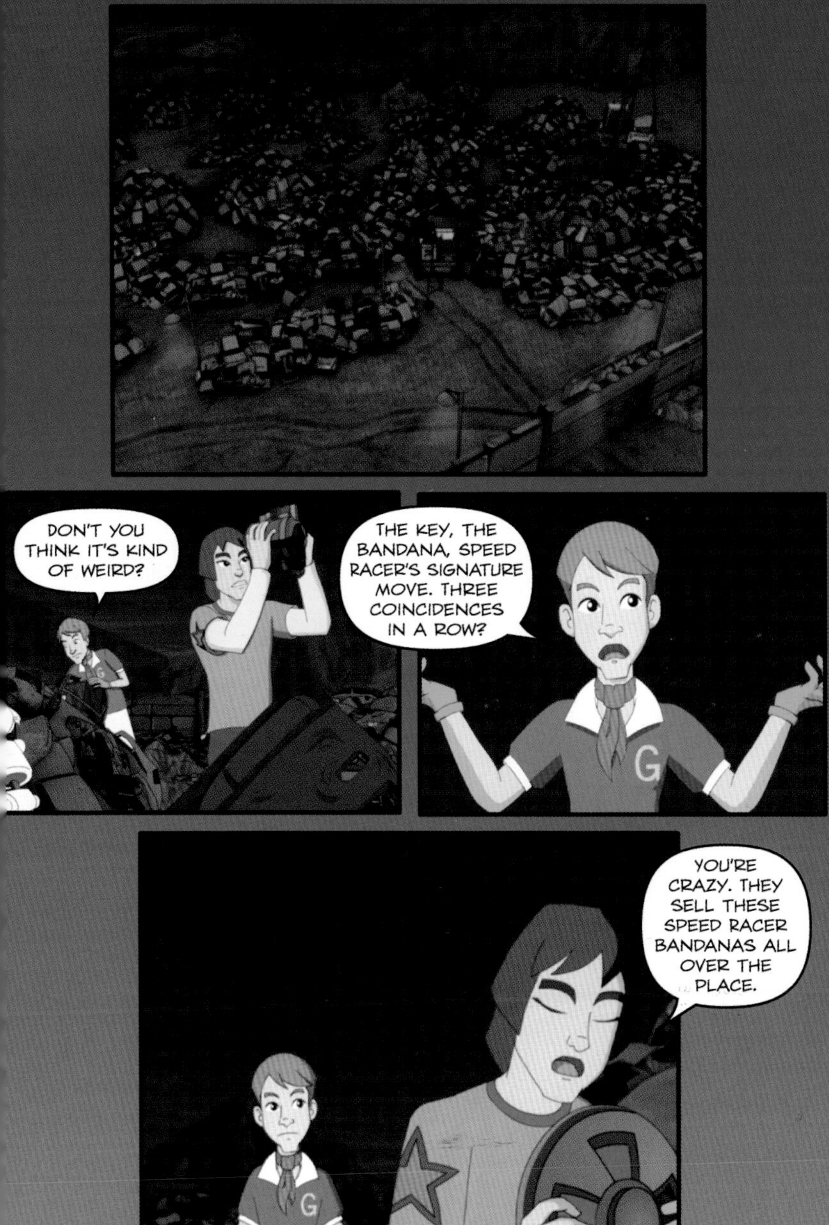
DON'T YOU THINK IT'S KIND OF WEIRD?
THE KEY, THE BANDANA, SPEED RACER'S SIGNATURE MOVE. THREE COINCIDENCES IN A ROW?
YOU'RE CRAZY. THEY SELL THESE SPEED RACER BANDANAS ALL OVER THE PLACE.

HUH?!

WITHOUT WARNING, THE KEY AROUND SPEED'S NECK BEGINS TO GLOW.

OKAY, THAT'S *WEIRD!*

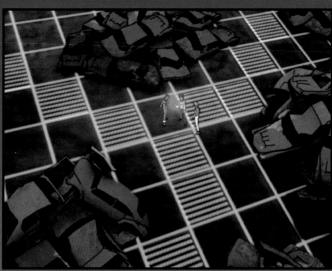

COOL! IT'S A THREE DIMENSIONAL HOLOGRAPHIC PROJECTION.

I THINK IT'S SOME KIND OF MAP. SEE THE RED MARKINGS?

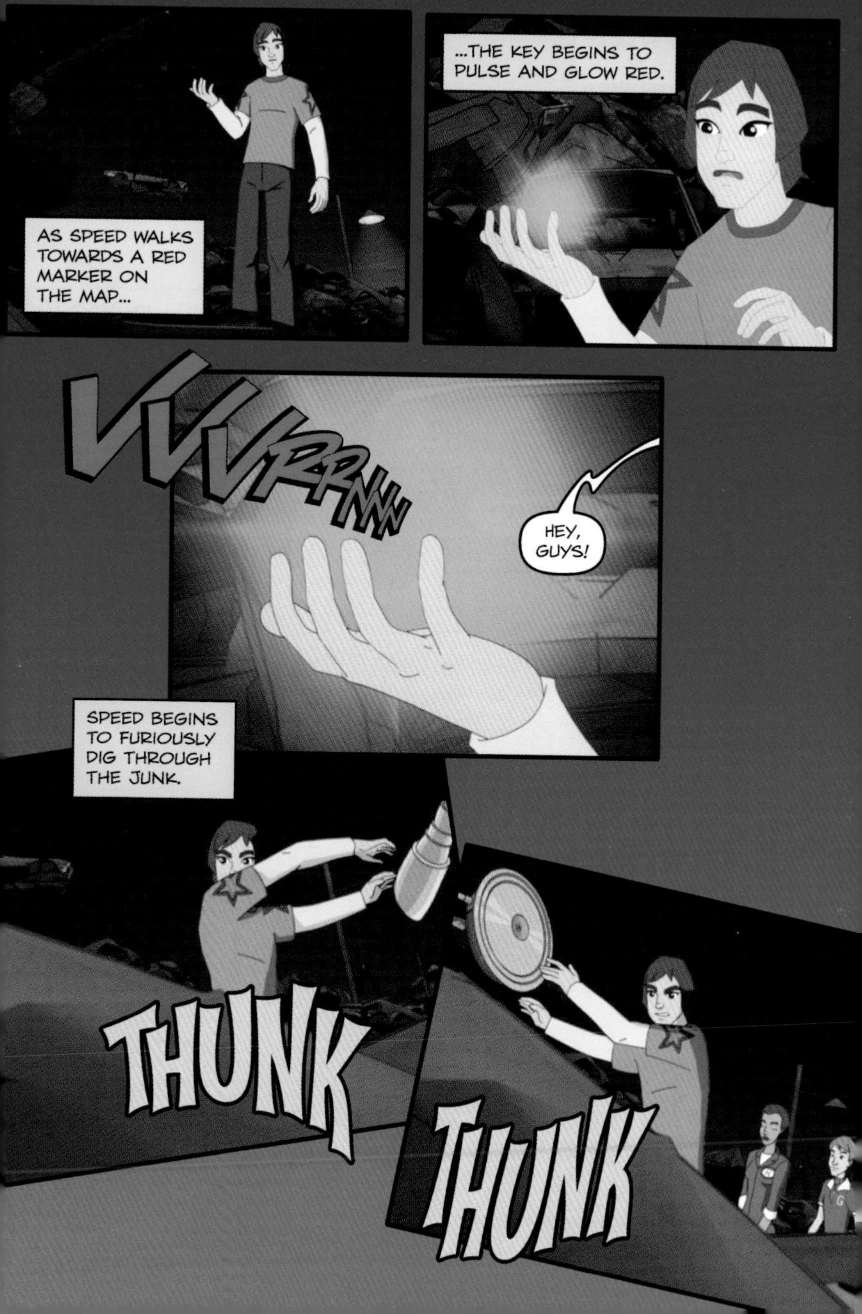
AS SPEED WALKS TOWARDS A RED MARKER ON THE MAP...
...THE KEY BEGINS TO PULSE AND GLOW RED.
VVVRRRNNN
HEY, GUYS!
SPEED BEGINS TO FURIOUSLY DIG THROUGH THE JUNK.
THUNK
THUNK

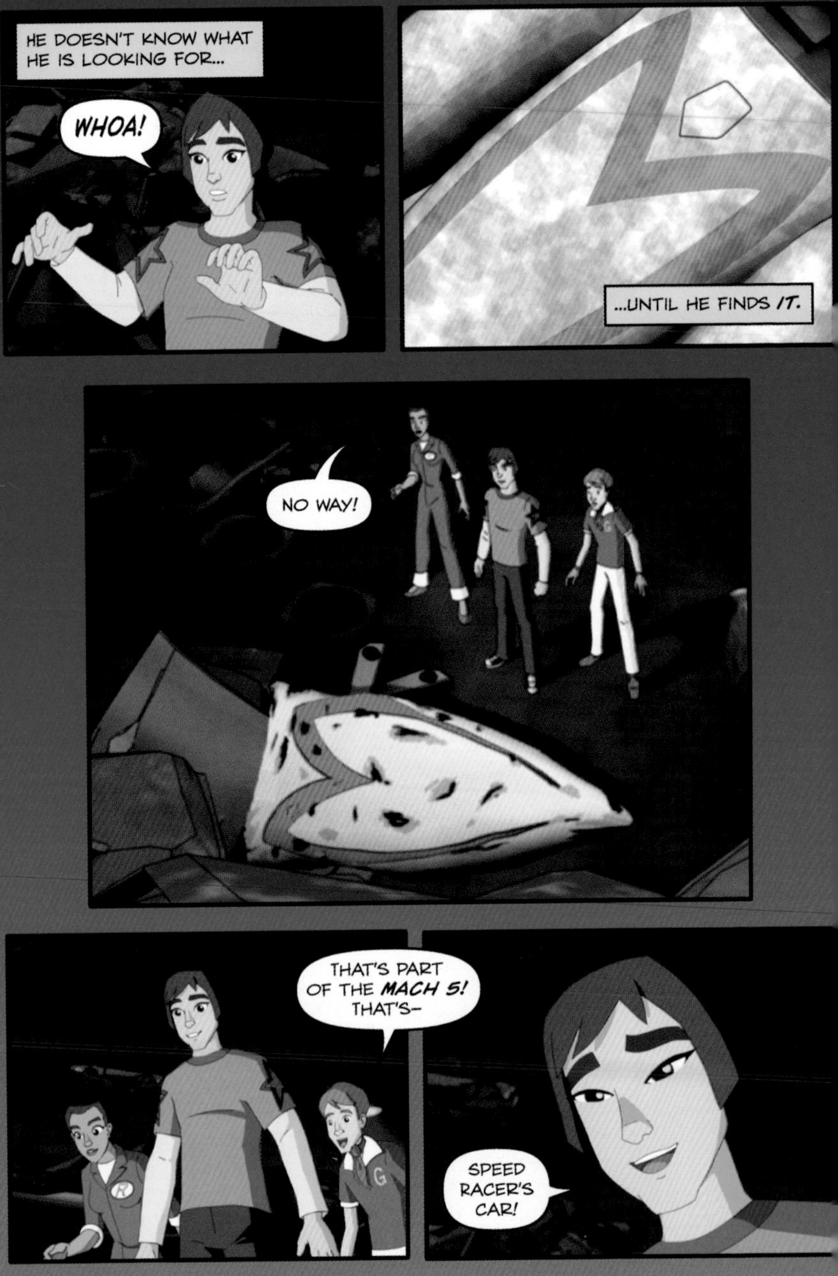
HE DOESN'T KNOW WHAT HE IS LOOKING FOR...
WHOA!
...UNTIL HE FINDS *IT.*
NO WAY!
THAT'S PART OF THE *MACH 5!* THAT'S–
SPEED RACER'S CAR!

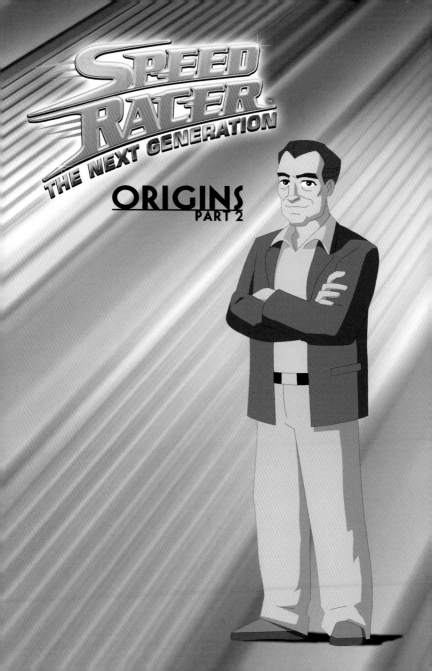

SPEED RACER
THE NEXT GENERATION

ORIGINS
PART 2

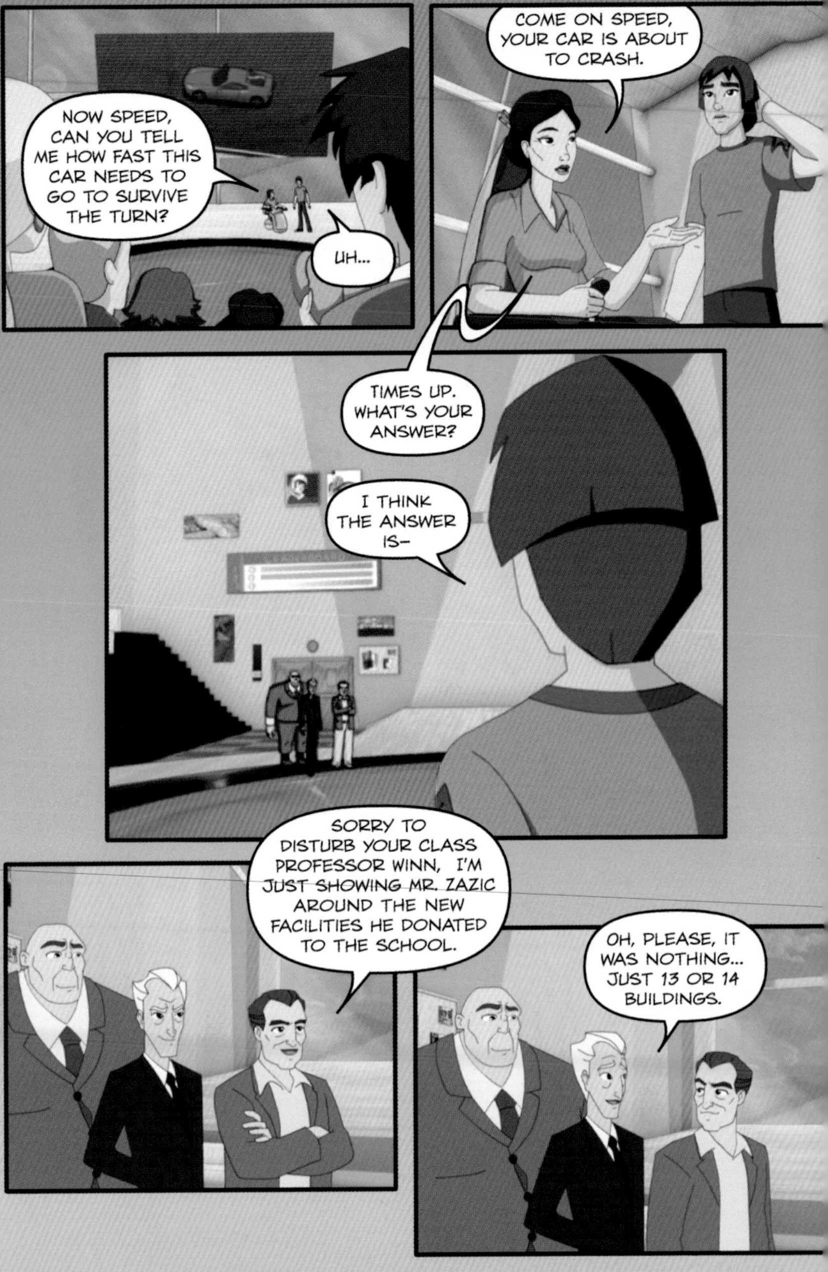
NOW SPEED, CAN YOU TELL ME HOW FAST THIS CAR NEEDS TO GO TO SURVIVE THE TURN?
UH...
COME ON SPEED, YOUR CAR IS ABOUT TO CRASH.
TIMES UP. WHAT'S YOUR ANSWER?
I THINK THE ANSWER IS–
SORRY TO DISTURB YOUR CLASS PROFESSOR WINN, I'M JUST SHOWING MR. ZAZIC AROUND THE NEW FACILITIES HE DONATED TO THE SCHOOL.
OH, PLEASE, IT WAS NOTHING... JUST 13 OR 14 BUILDINGS.

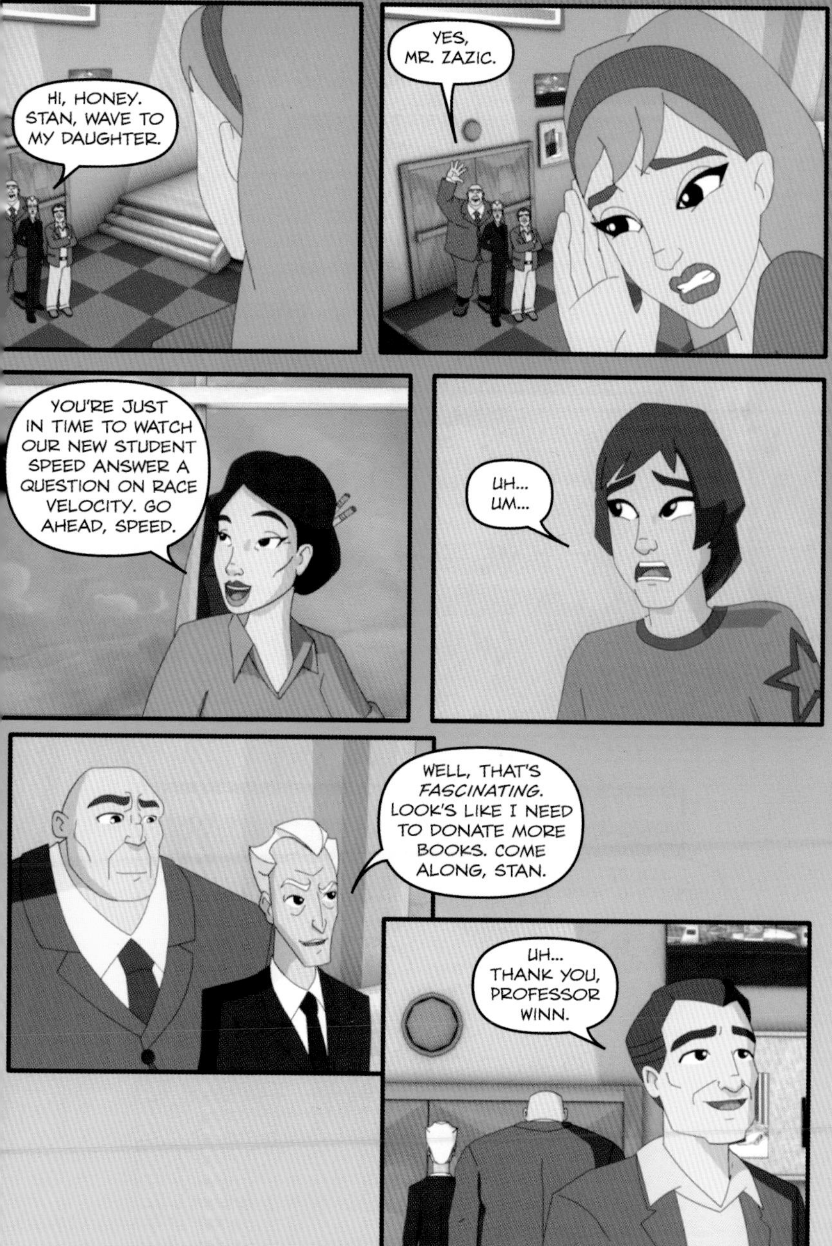
HI, HONEY. STAN, WAVE TO MY DAUGHTER.
YES, MR. ZAZIC.
YOU'RE JUST IN TIME TO WATCH OUR NEW STUDENT SPEED ANSWER A QUESTION ON RACE VELOCITY. GO AHEAD, SPEED.
UH... UM...
WELL, THAT'S *FASCINATING*. LOOK'S LIKE I NEED TO DONATE MORE BOOKS. COME ALONG, STAN.
UH... THANK YOU, PROFESSOR WINN.

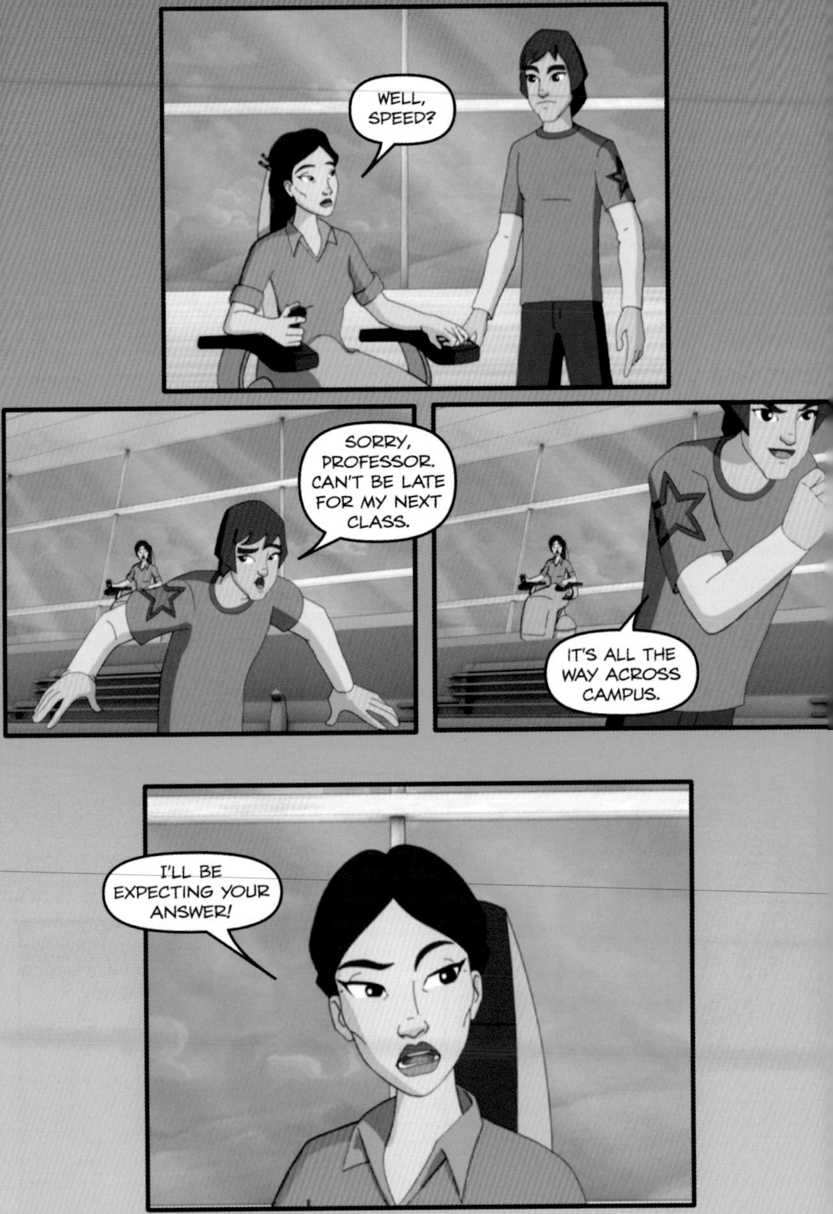
WELL, SPEED?
SORRY, PROFESSOR. CAN'T BE LATE FOR MY NEXT CLASS.
IT'S ALL THE WAY ACROSS CAMPUS.
I'LL BE EXPECTING YOUR ANSWER!

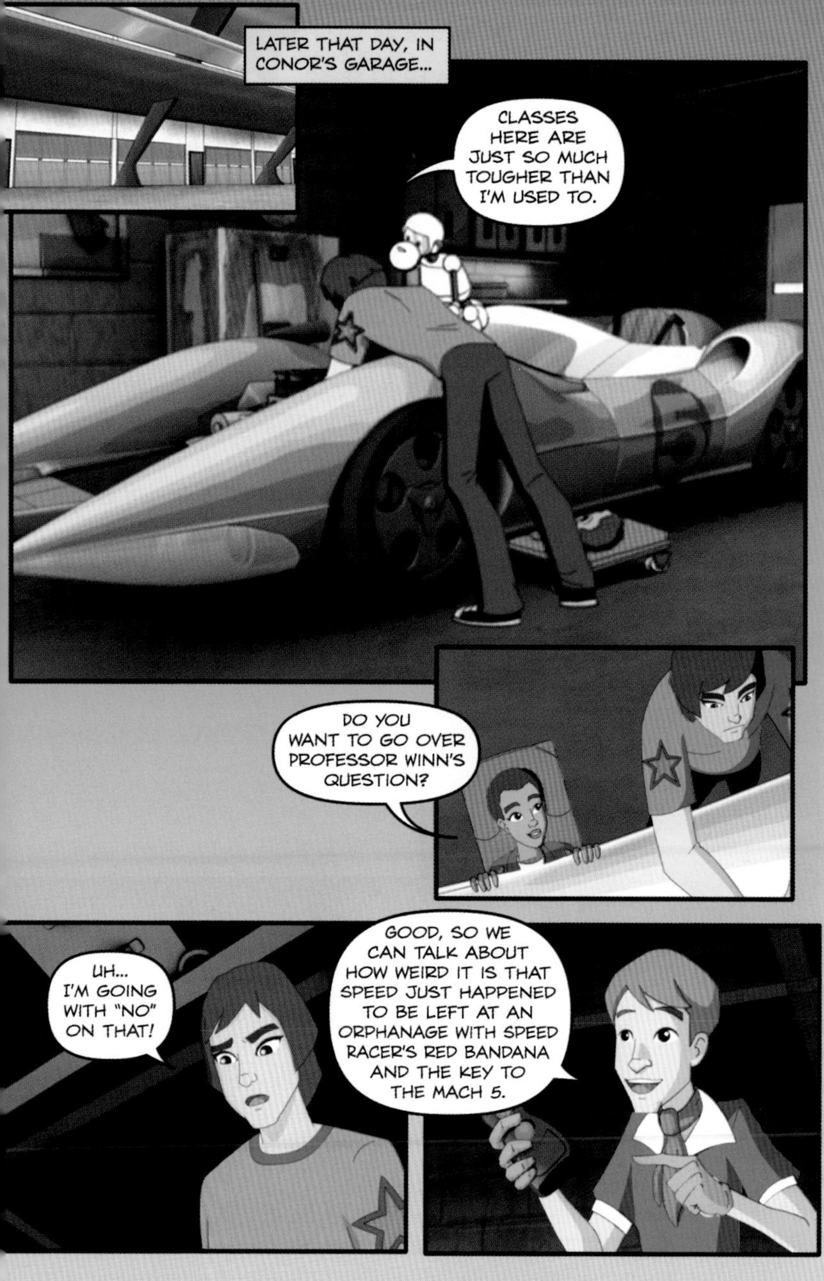
LATER THAT DAY, IN CONOR'S GARAGE...
CLASSES HERE ARE JUST SO MUCH TOUGHER THAN I'M USED TO.
DO YOU WANT TO GO OVER PROFESSOR WINN'S QUESTION?
UH... I'M GOING WITH "NO" ON THAT!
GOOD, SO WE CAN TALK ABOUT HOW WEIRD IT IS THAT SPEED JUST HAPPENED TO BE LEFT AT AN ORPHANAGE WITH SPEED RACER'S RED BANDANA AND THE KEY TO THE MACH 5.

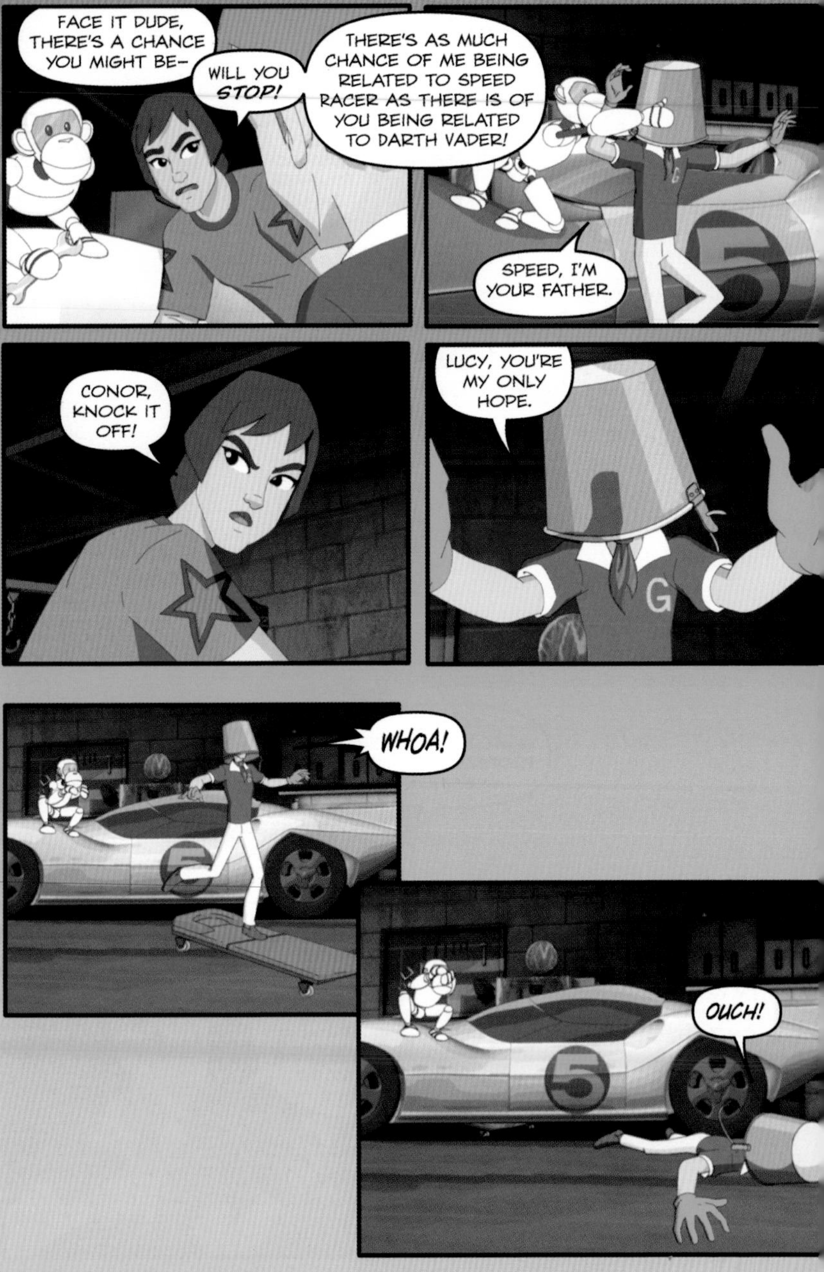
FACE IT DUDE, THERE'S A CHANCE YOU MIGHT BE–
WILL YOU *STOP!*
THERE'S AS MUCH CHANCE OF ME BEING RELATED TO SPEED RACER AS THERE IS OF YOU BEING RELATED TO DARTH VADER!
SPEED, I'M YOUR FATHER.
CONOR, KNOCK IT OFF!
LUCY, YOU'RE MY ONLY HOPE.
WHOA!
OUCH!

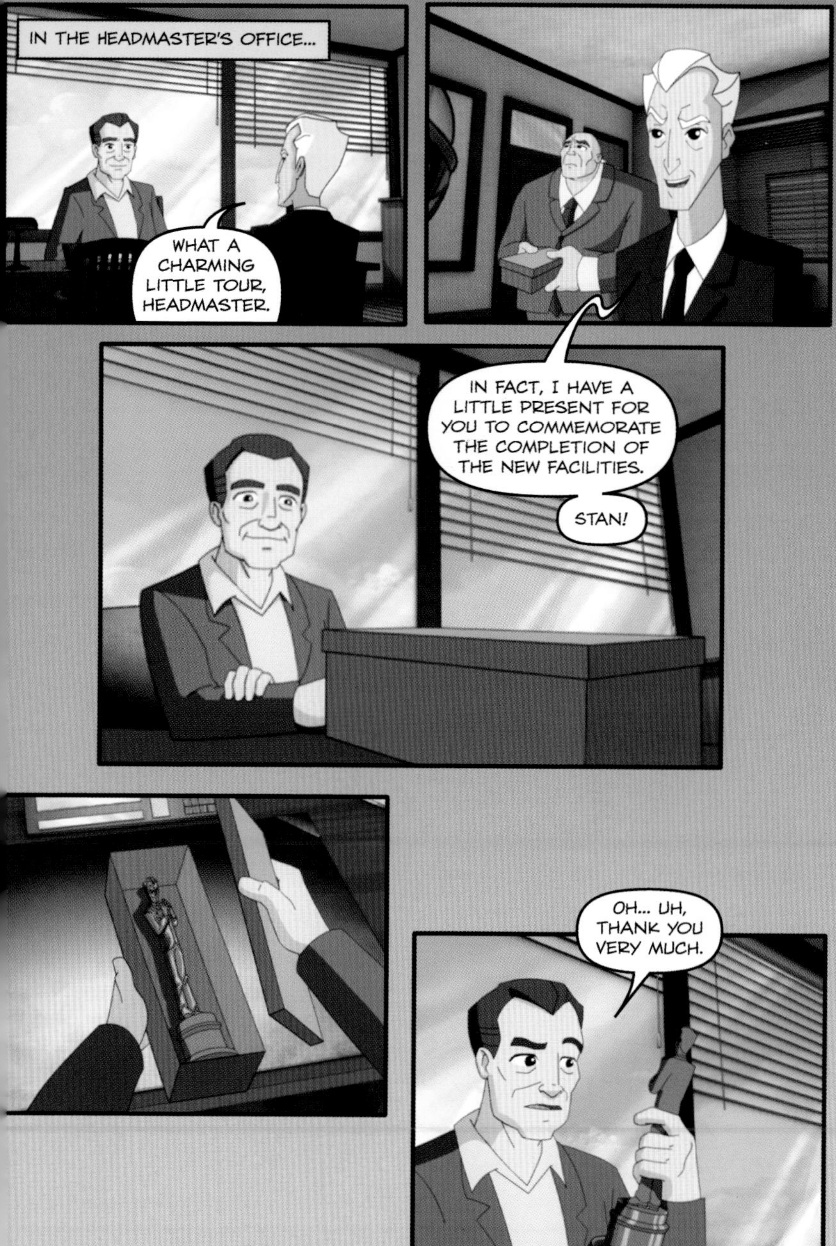
IN THE HEADMASTER'S OFFICE...
WHAT A CHARMING LITTLE TOUR, HEADMASTER.
IN FACT, I HAVE A LITTLE PRESENT FOR YOU TO COMMEMORATE THE COMPLETION OF THE NEW FACILITIES.
STAN!
OH... UH, THANK YOU VERY MUCH.

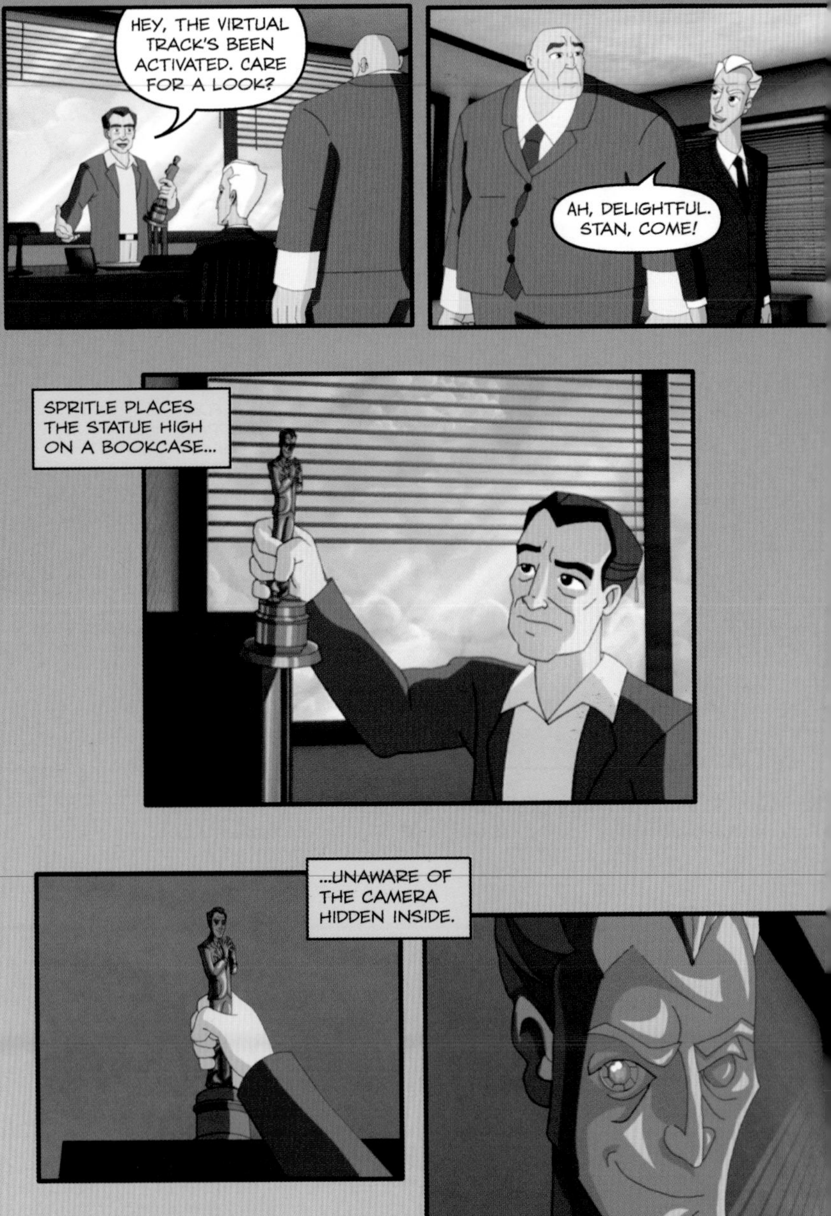
HEY, THE VIRTUAL TRACK'S BEEN ACTIVATED. CARE FOR A LOOK?
AH, DELIGHTFUL. STAN, COME!
SPRITLE PLACES THE STATUE HIGH ON A BOOKCASE...
...UNAWARE OF THE CAMERA HIDDEN INSIDE.

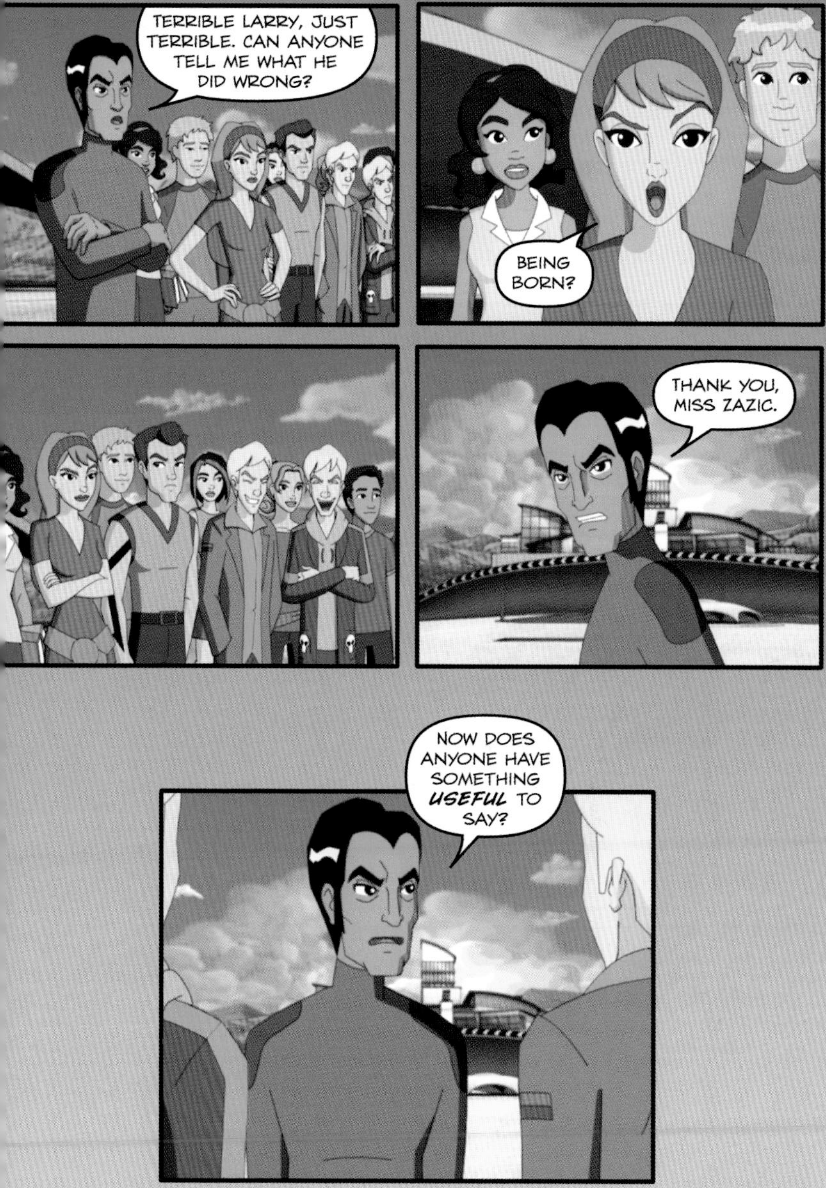
TERRIBLE LARRY, JUST TERRIBLE. CAN ANYONE TELL ME WHAT HE DID WRONG?
BEING BORN?
THANK YOU, MISS ZAZIC.
NOW DOES ANYONE HAVE SOMETHING *USEFUL* TO SAY?

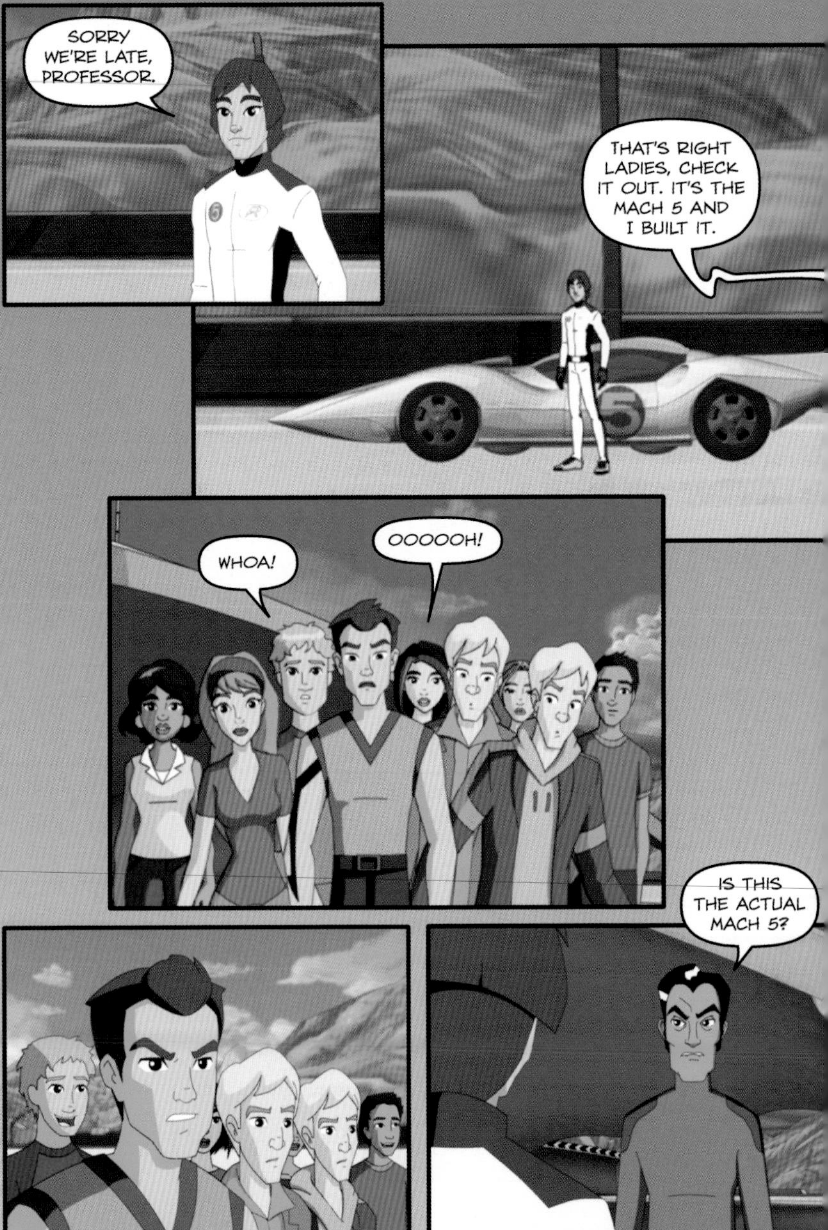
SORRY WE'RE LATE, PROFESSOR.
THAT'S RIGHT LADIES, CHECK IT OUT. IT'S THE MACH 5 AND I BUILT IT.
WHOA!
OOOOOH!
IS THIS THE ACTUAL MACH 5?

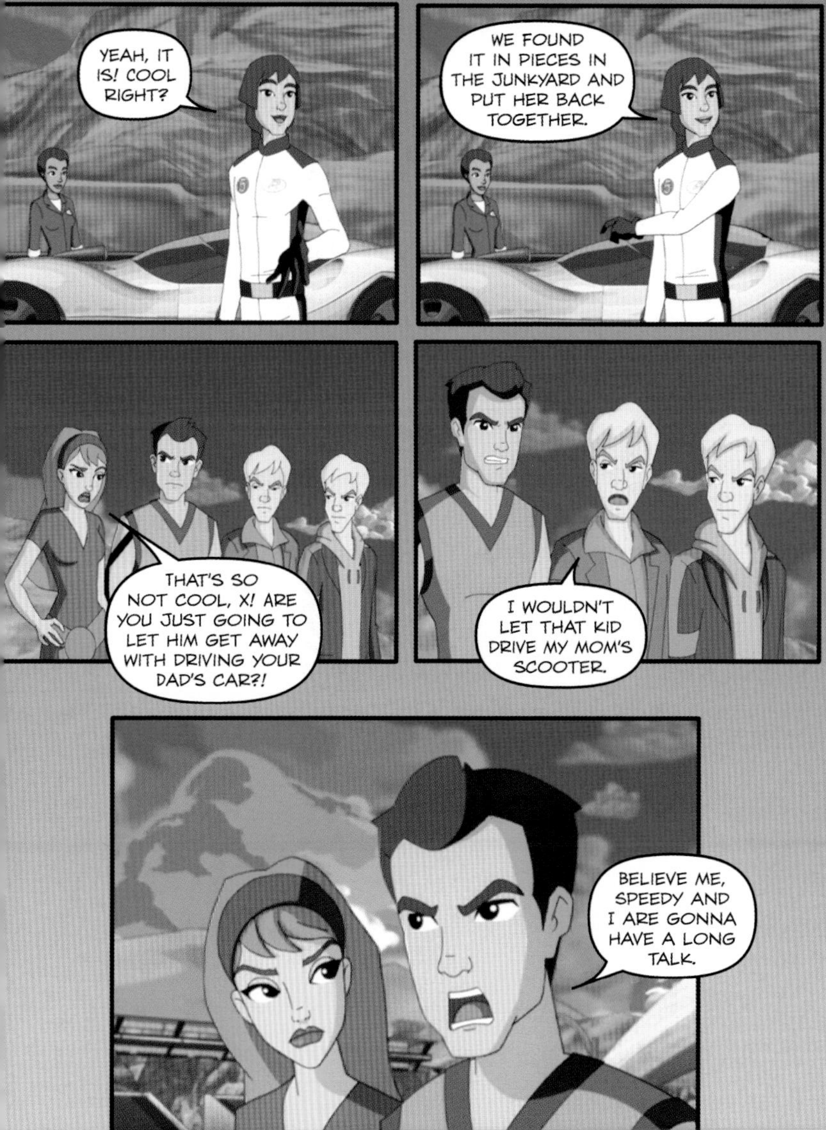

YEAH, IT IS! COOL RIGHT?
WE FOUND IT IN PIECES IN THE JUNKYARD AND PUT HER BACK TOGETHER.
THAT'S SO NOT COOL, X! ARE YOU JUST GOING TO LET HIM GET AWAY WITH DRIVING YOUR DAD'S CAR?!
I WOULDN'T LET THAT KID DRIVE MY MOM'S SCOOTER.
BELIEVE ME, SPEEDY AND I ARE GONNA HAVE A LONG TALK.

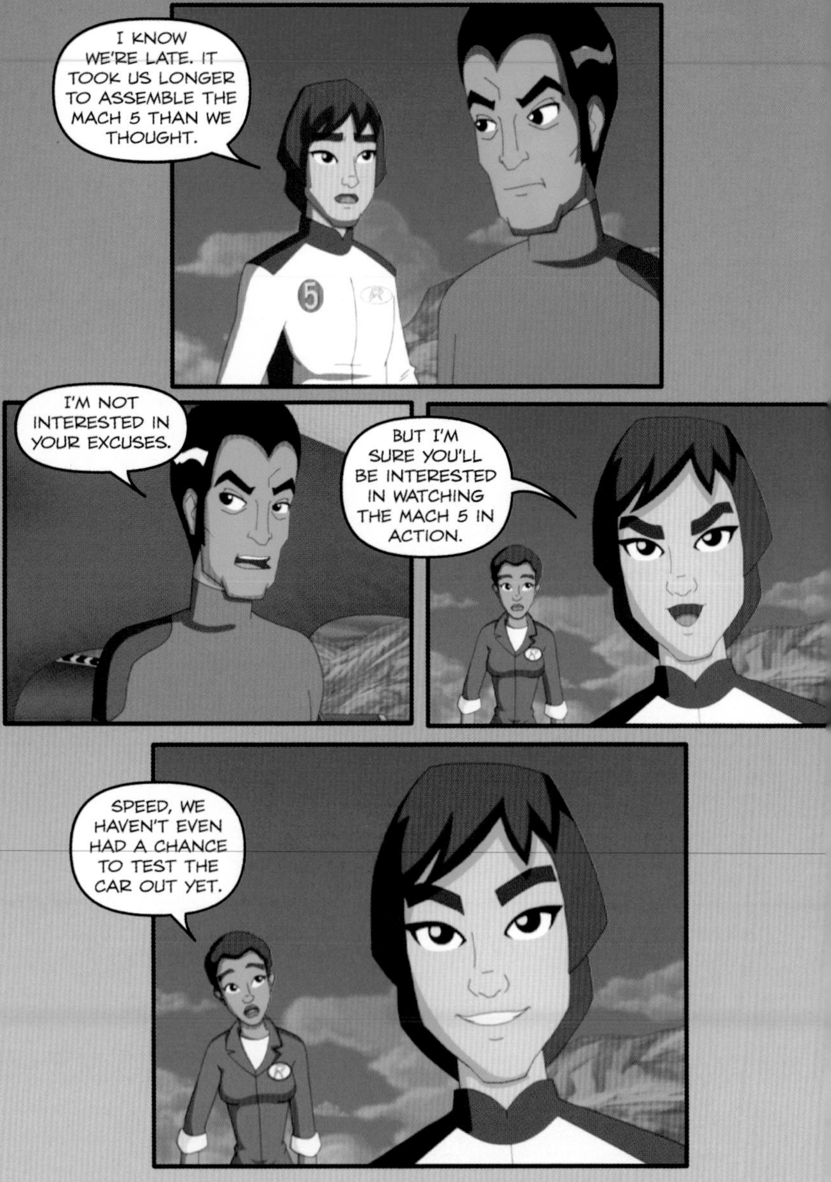
I KNOW WE'RE LATE. IT TOOK US LONGER TO ASSEMBLE THE MACH 5 THAN WE THOUGHT.
I'M NOT INTERESTED IN YOUR EXCUSES.
BUT I'M SURE YOU'LL BE INTERESTED IN WATCHING THE MACH 5 IN ACTION.
SPEED, WE HAVEN'T EVEN HAD A CHANCE TO TEST THE CAR OUT YET.

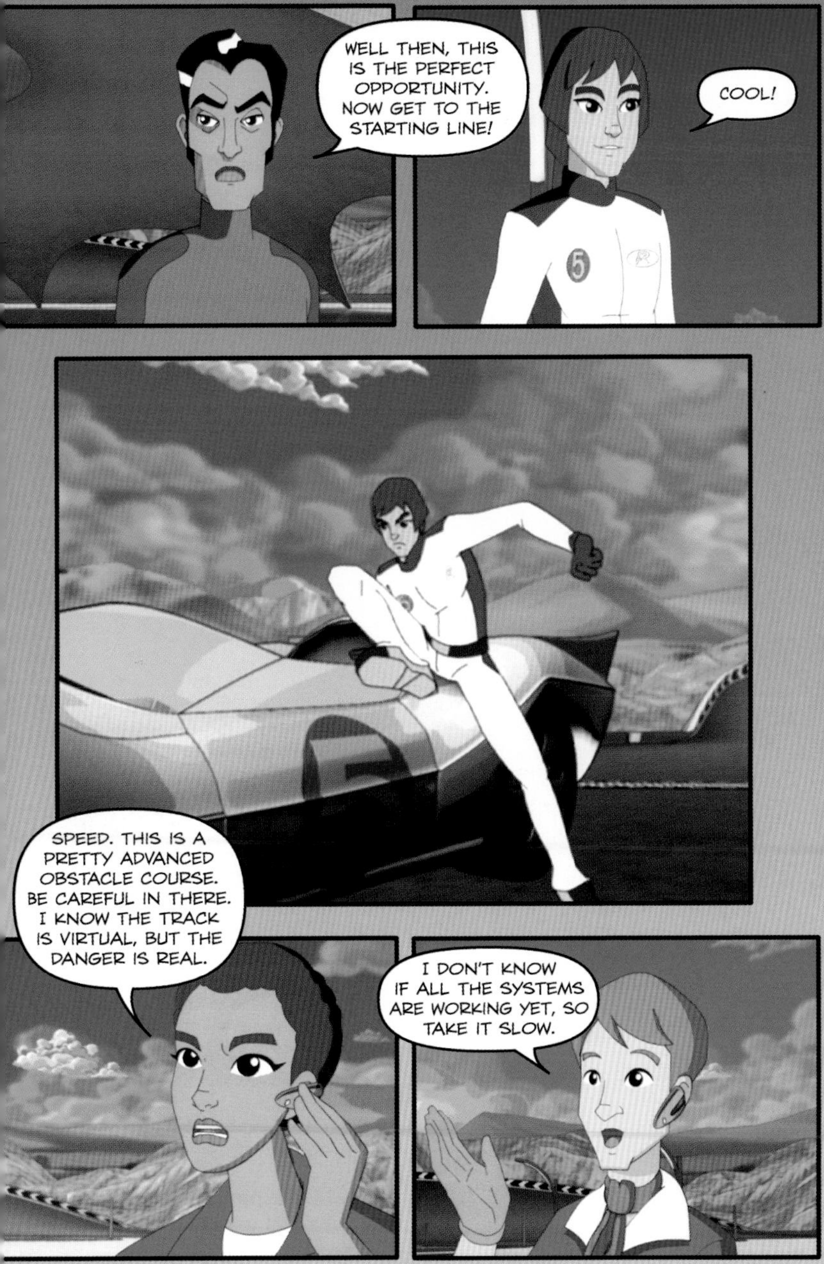
WELL THEN, THIS IS THE PERFECT OPPORTUNITY. NOW GET TO THE STARTING LINE!
COOL!
SPEED. THIS IS A PRETTY ADVANCED OBSTACLE COURSE. BE CAREFUL IN THERE. I KNOW THE TRACK IS VIRTUAL, BUT THE DANGER IS REAL.
I DON'T KNOW IF ALL THE SYSTEMS ARE WORKING YET, SO TAKE IT SLOW.

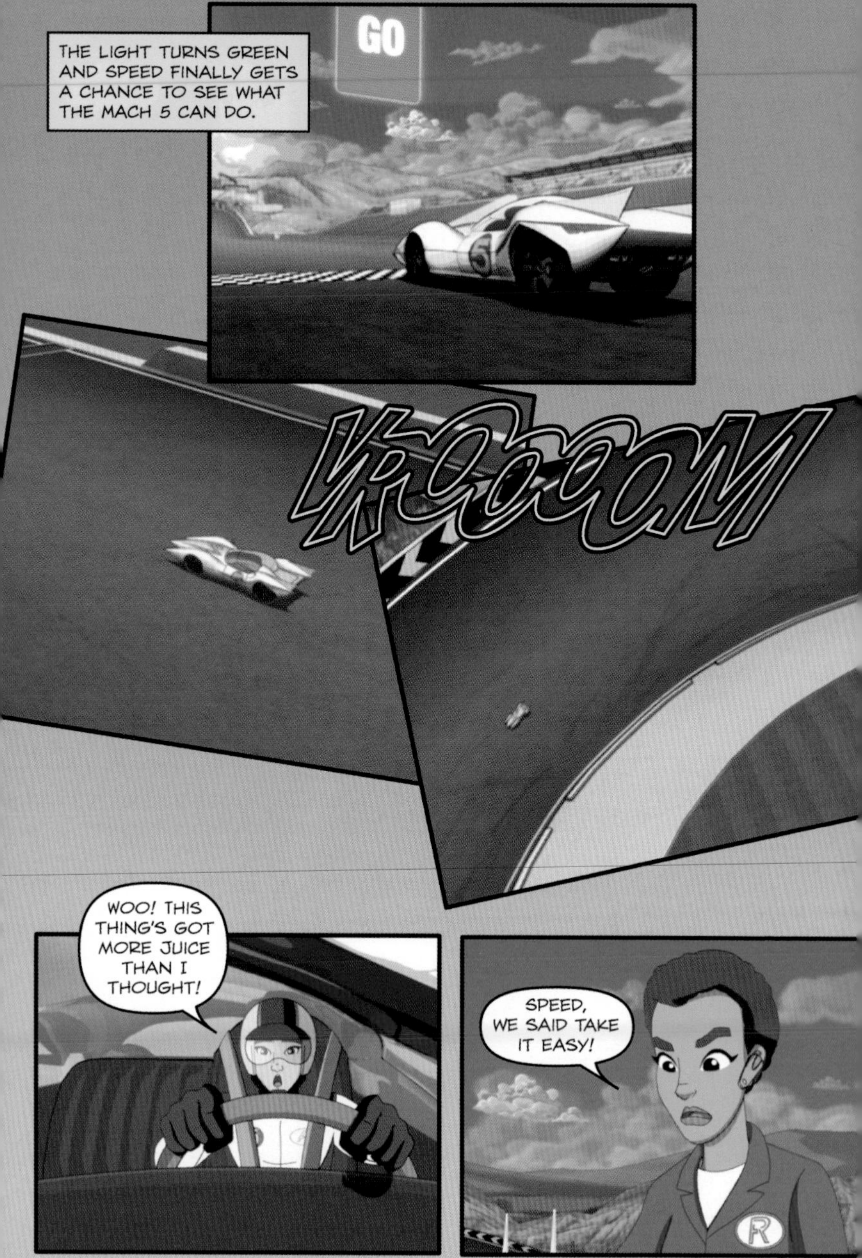
GO
THE LIGHT TURNS GREEN AND SPEED FINALLY GETS A CHANCE TO SEE WHAT THE MACH 5 CAN DO.
VROOOOOM
WOO! THIS THING'S GOT MORE JUICE THAN I THOUGHT!
SPEED, WE SAID TAKE IT EASY!

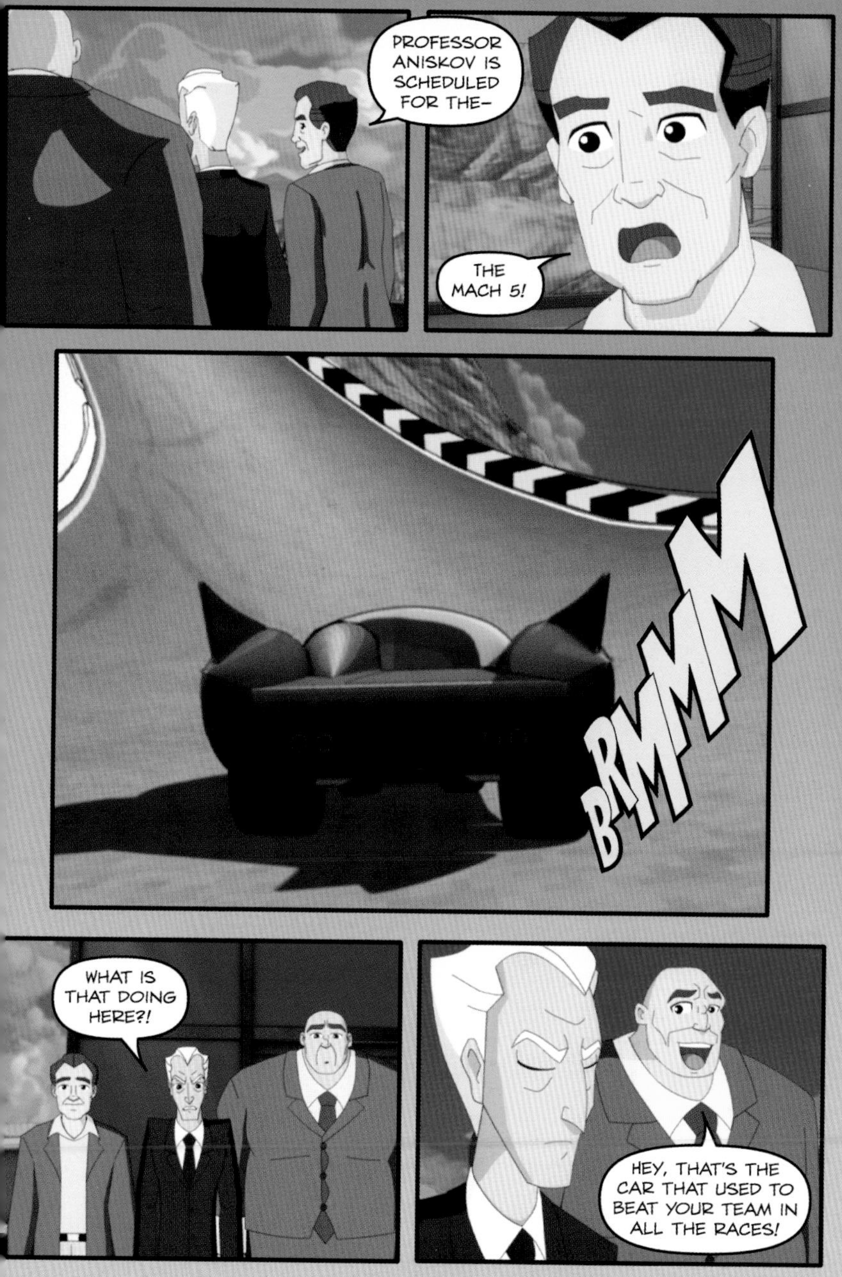
PROFESSOR ANISKOV IS SCHEDULED FOR THE-
THE MACH 5!
BRMMM
WHAT IS THAT DOING HERE?!
HEY, THAT'S THE CAR THAT USED TO BEAT YOUR TEAM IN ALL THE RACES!

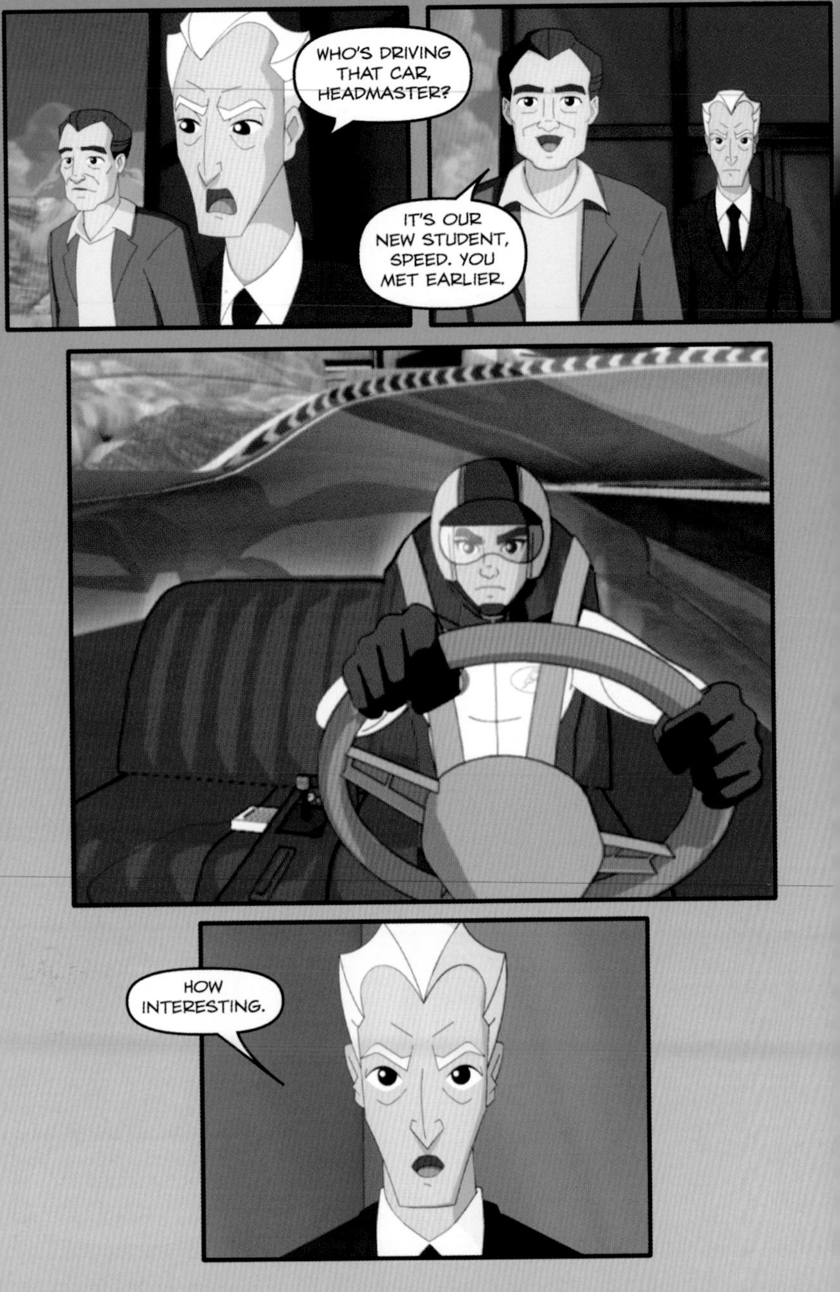
WHO'S DRIVING THAT CAR, HEADMASTER?
IT'S OUR NEW STUDENT, SPEED. YOU MET EARLIER.
HOW INTERESTING.

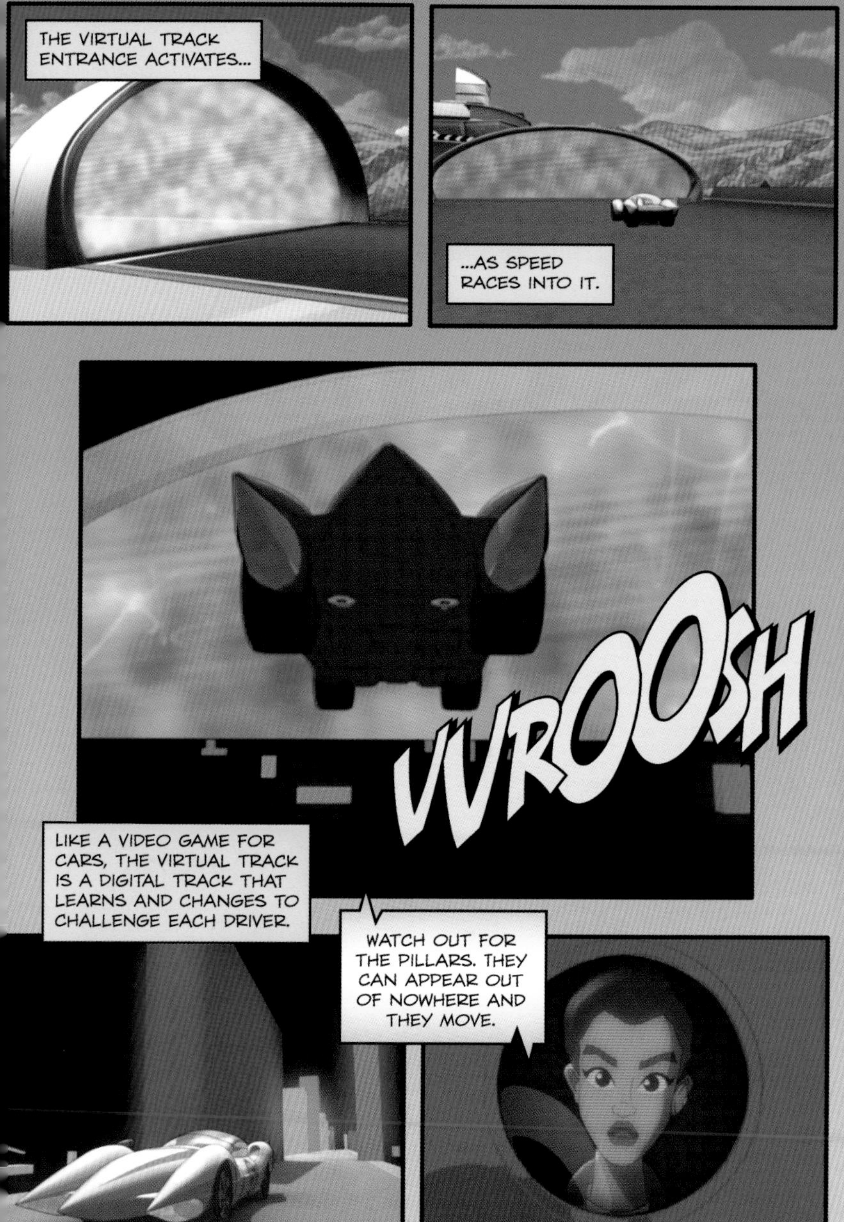
THE VIRTUAL TRACK ENTRANCE ACTIVATES...
...AS SPEED RACES INTO IT.
VVROOOSH
LIKE A VIDEO GAME FOR CARS, THE VIRTUAL TRACK IS A DIGITAL TRACK THAT LEARNS AND CHANGES TO CHALLENGE EACH DRIVER.
WATCH OUT FOR THE PILLARS. THEY CAN APPEAR OUT OF NOWHERE AND THEY MOVE.

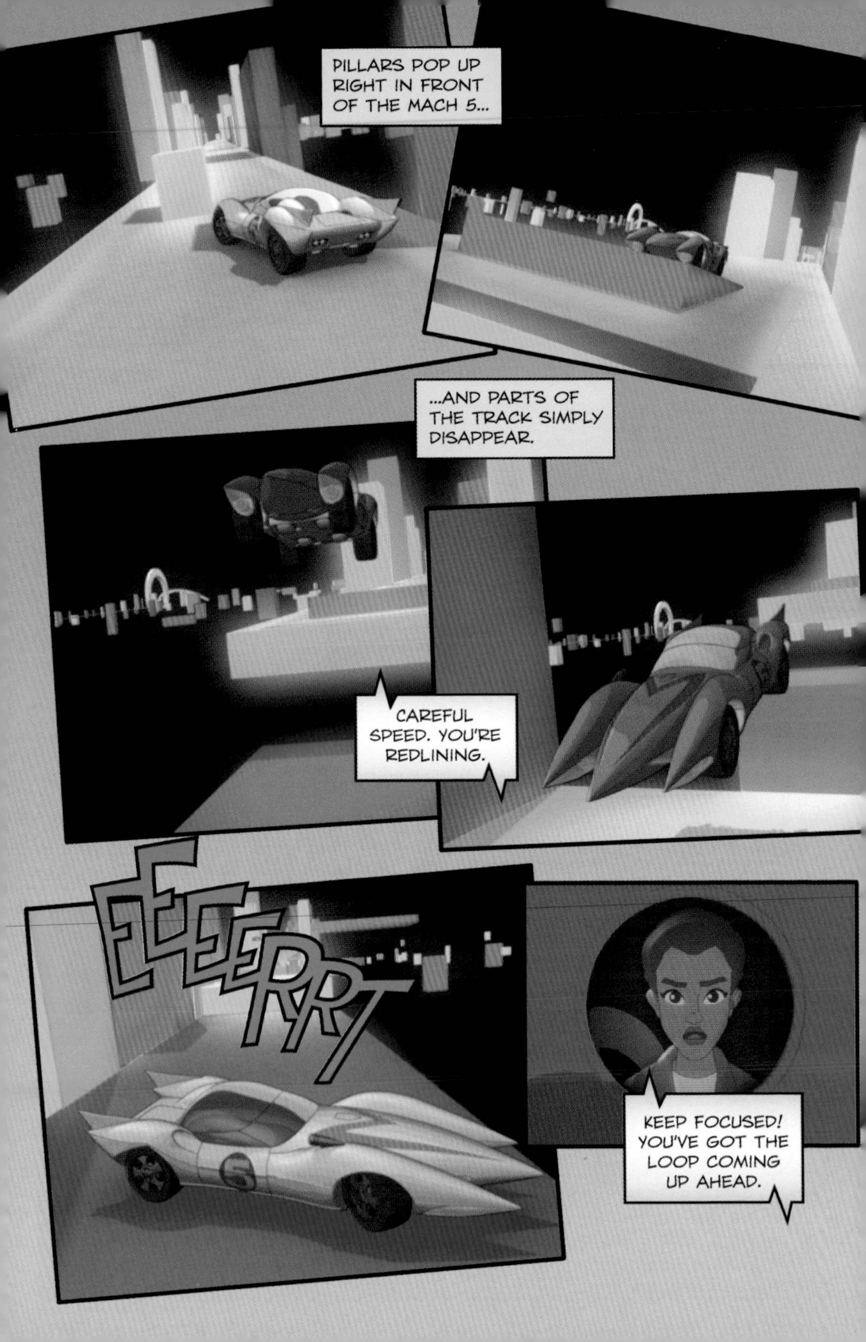
PILLARS POP UP RIGHT IN FRONT OF THE MACH 5...
...AND PARTS OF THE TRACK SIMPLY DISAPPEAR.
CAREFUL SPEED. YOU'RE REDLINING.
EEEERRT
KEEP FOCUSED! YOU'VE GOT THE LOOP COMING UP AHEAD.

THE LOOP? NO WAY!

SPEED, ACTIVATE THE SUPER-GRIP TREADS. LETTER B.

GOT IT.

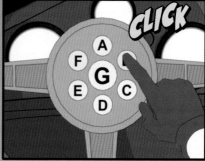

CLICK

A
F G C
E D

SQUAK SQUAK

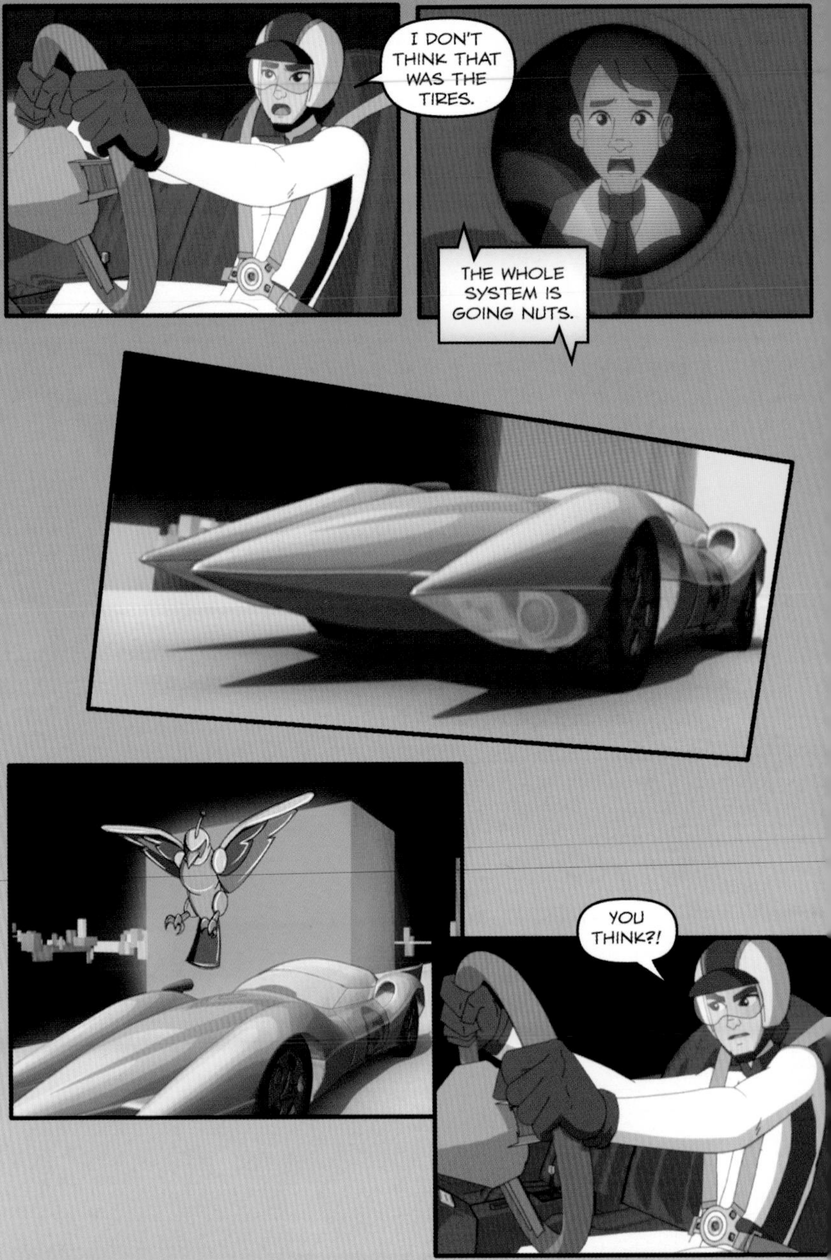
I DON'T THINK THAT WAS THE TIRES.
THE WHOLE SYSTEM IS GOING NUTS.
YOU THINK?!

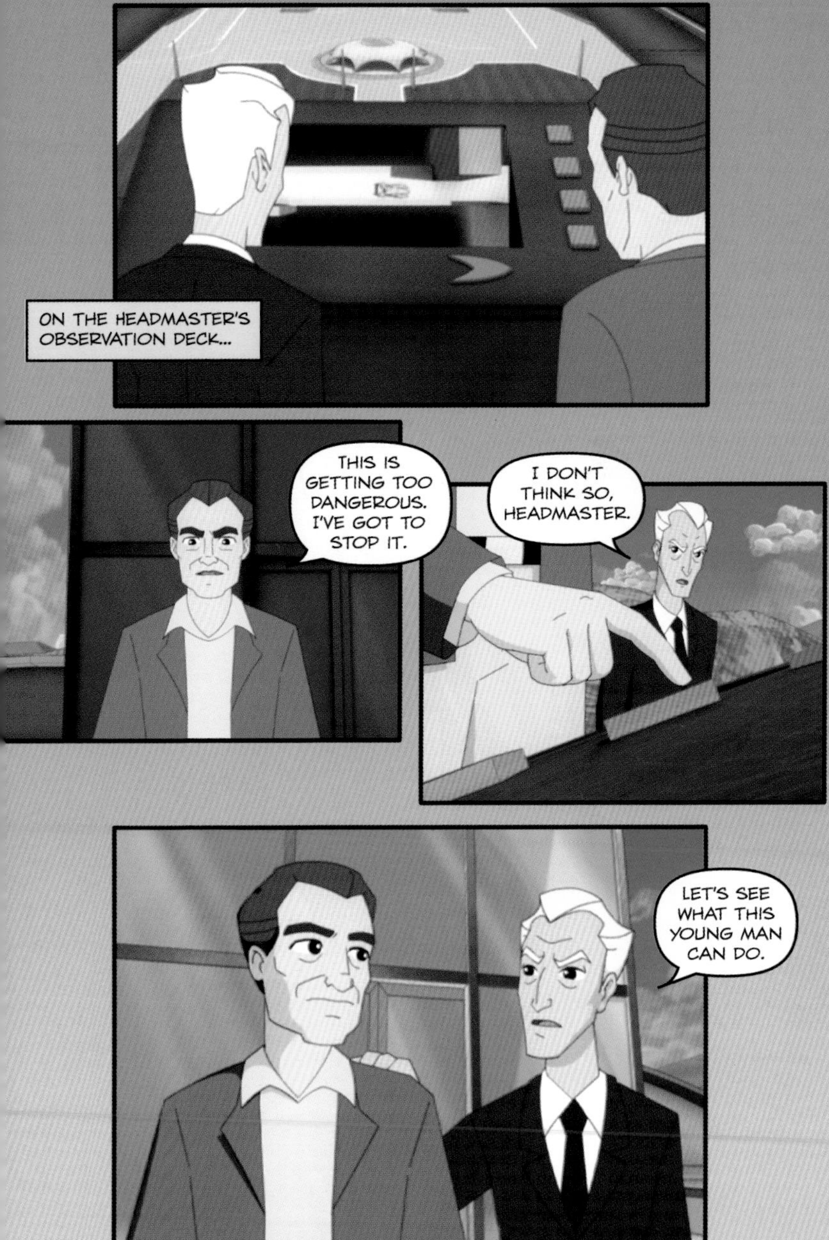
ON THE HEADMASTER'S OBSERVATION DECK...
THIS IS GETTING TOO DANGEROUS. I'VE GOT TO STOP IT.
I DON'T THINK SO, HEADMASTER.
LET'S SEE WHAT THIS YOUNG MAN CAN DO.

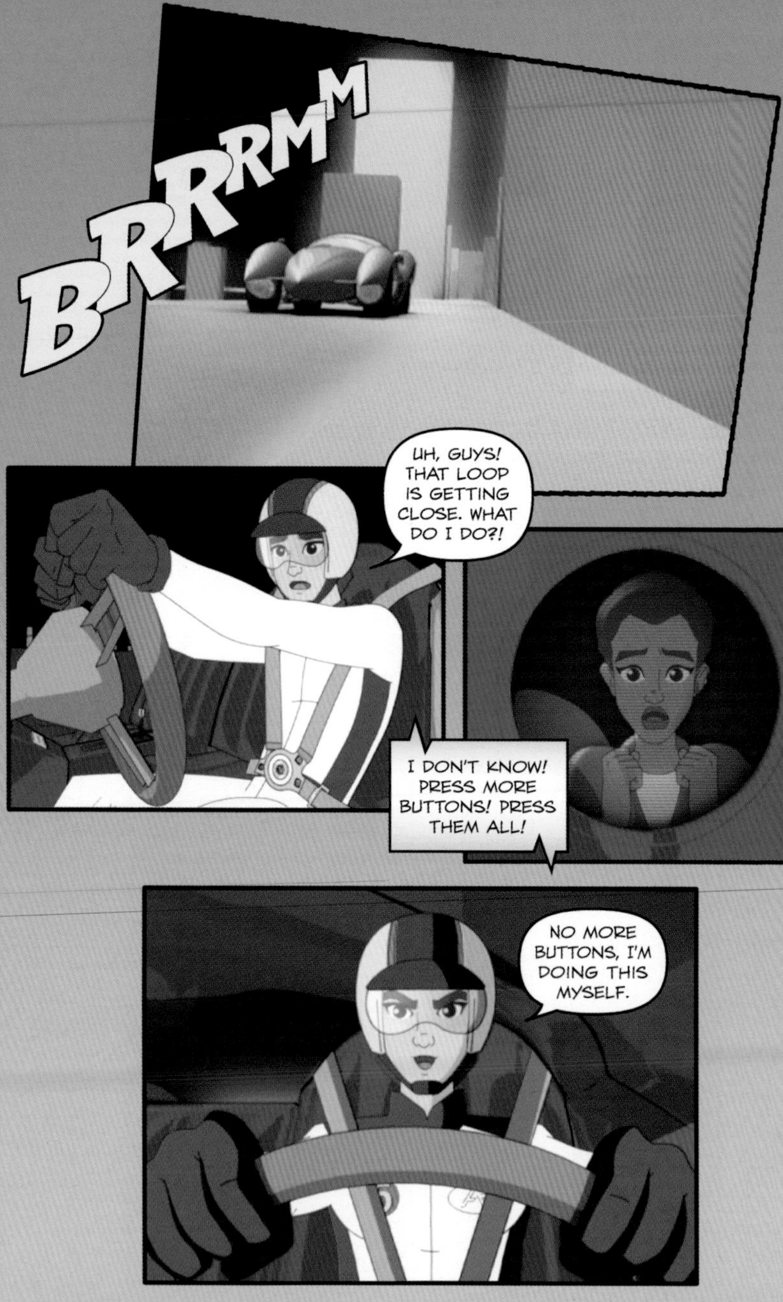
BRRRMM
UH, GUYS! THAT LOOP IS GETTING CLOSE. WHAT DO I DO?!
I DON'T KNOW! PRESS MORE BUTTONS! PRESS THEM ALL!
NO MORE BUTTONS, I'M DOING THIS MYSELF.

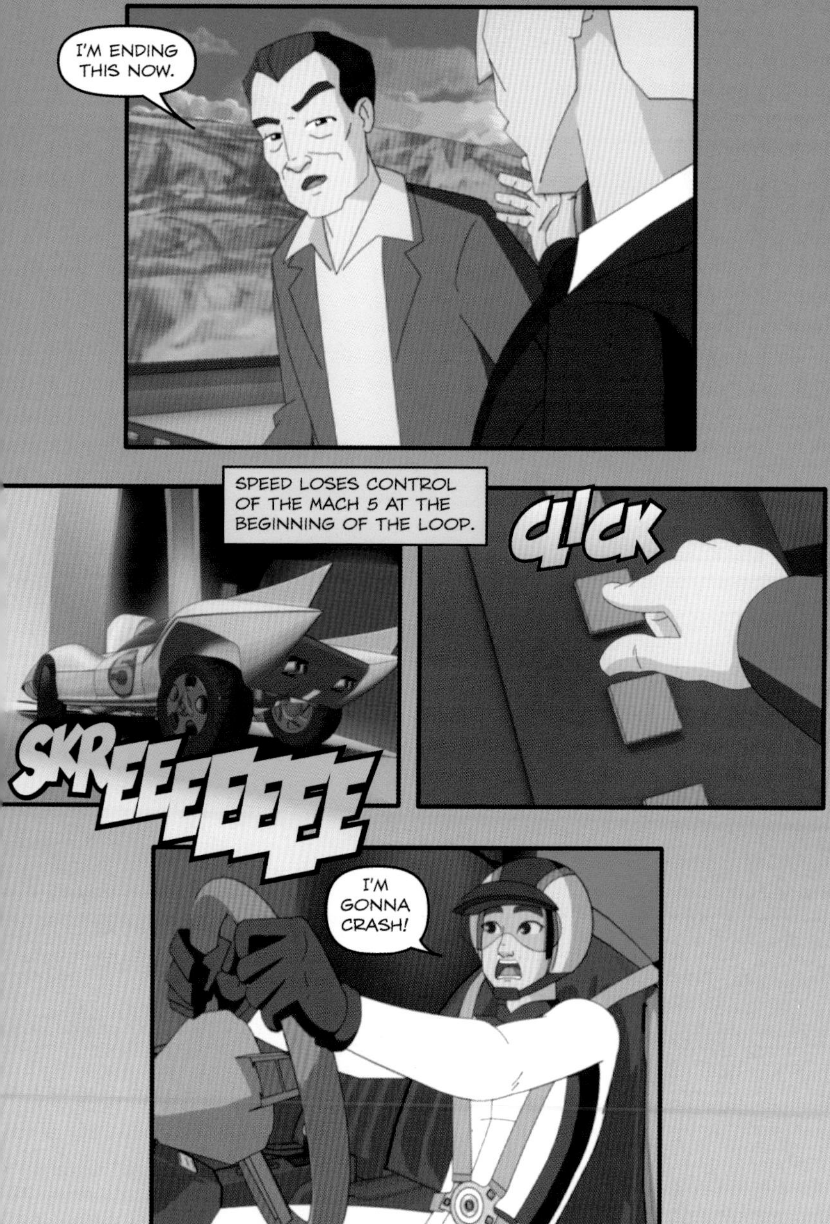
I'M ENDING THIS NOW.
SPEED LOSES CONTROL OF THE MACH 5 AT THE BEGINNING OF THE LOOP.
SKREEEEEEE
CLICK
I'M GONNA CRASH!

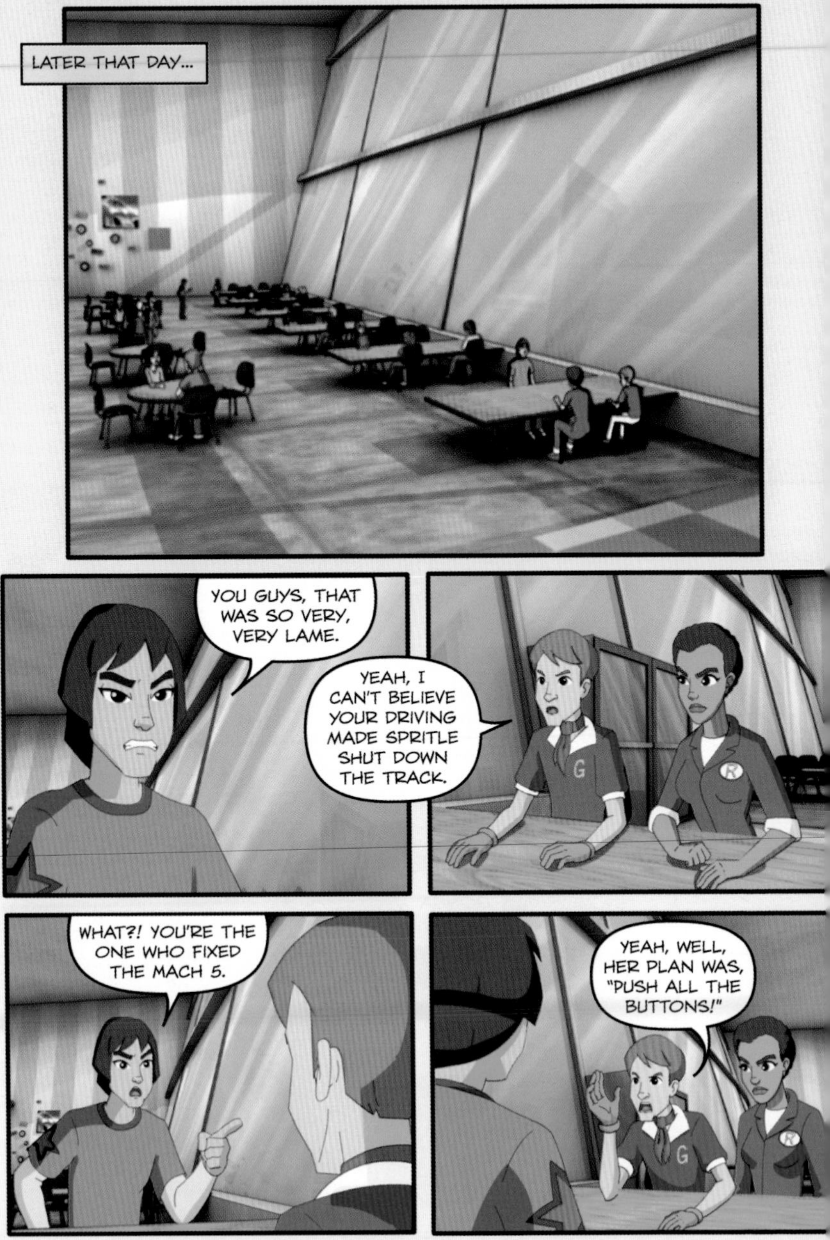
LATER THAT DAY...
YOU GUYS, THAT WAS SO VERY, VERY LAME.
YEAH, I CAN'T BELIEVE YOUR DRIVING MADE SPRITLE SHUT DOWN THE TRACK.
WHAT?! YOU'RE THE ONE WHO FIXED THE MACH 5.
YEAH, WELL, HER PLAN WAS, "PUSH ALL THE BUTTONS!"

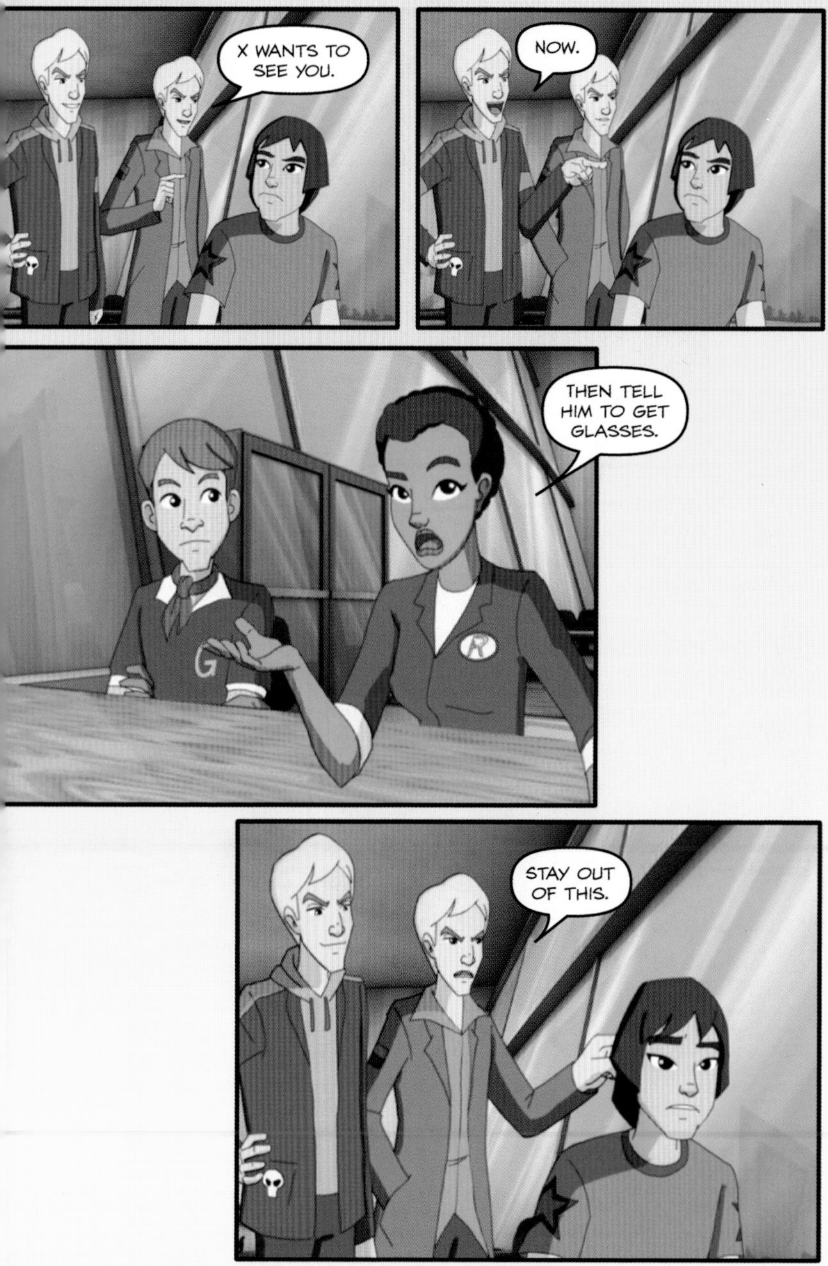
X WANTS TO SEE YOU.
NOW.
THEN TELL HIM TO GET GLASSES.
STAY OUT OF THIS.

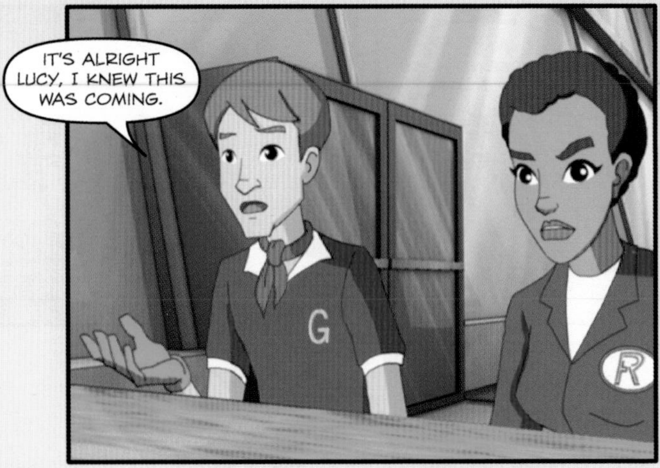
IT'S ALRIGHT LUCY, I KNEW THIS WAS COMING.

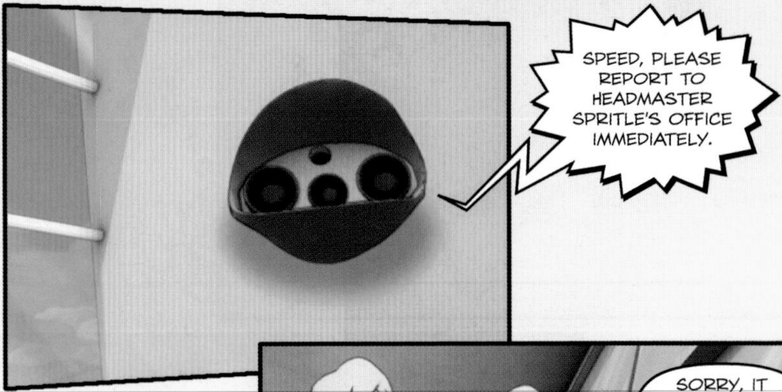
SPEED, PLEASE REPORT TO HEADMASTER SPRITLE'S OFFICE IMMEDIATELY.

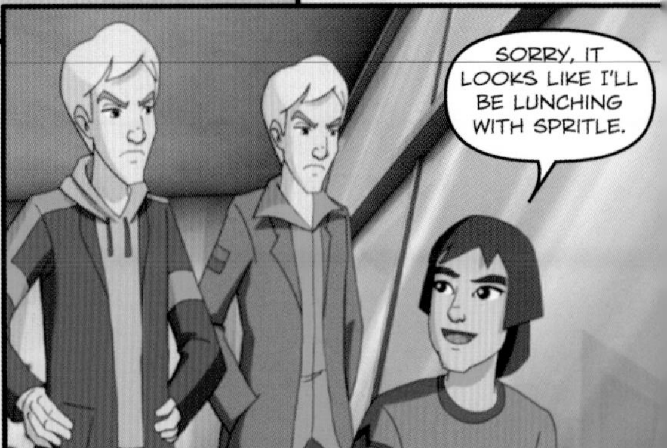
SORRY, IT LOOKS LIKE I'LL BE LUNCHING WITH SPRITLE.

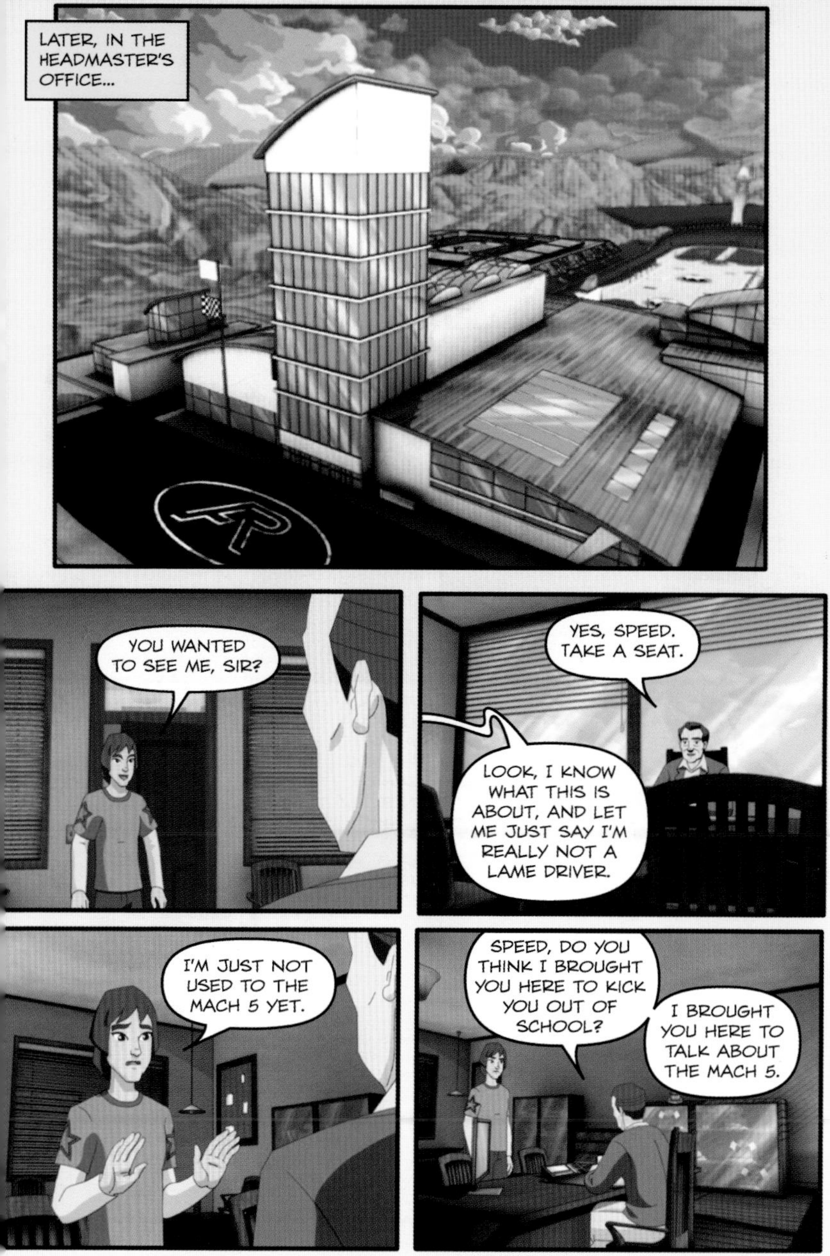
LATER, IN THE HEADMASTER'S OFFICE...
YOU WANTED TO SEE ME, SIR?
YES, SPEED. TAKE A SEAT.
LOOK, I KNOW WHAT THIS IS ABOUT, AND LET ME JUST SAY I'M REALLY NOT A LAME DRIVER.
I'M JUST NOT USED TO THE MACH 5 YET.
SPEED, DO YOU THINK I BROUGHT YOU HERE TO KICK YOU OUT OF SCHOOL?
I BROUGHT YOU HERE TO TALK ABOUT THE MACH 5.

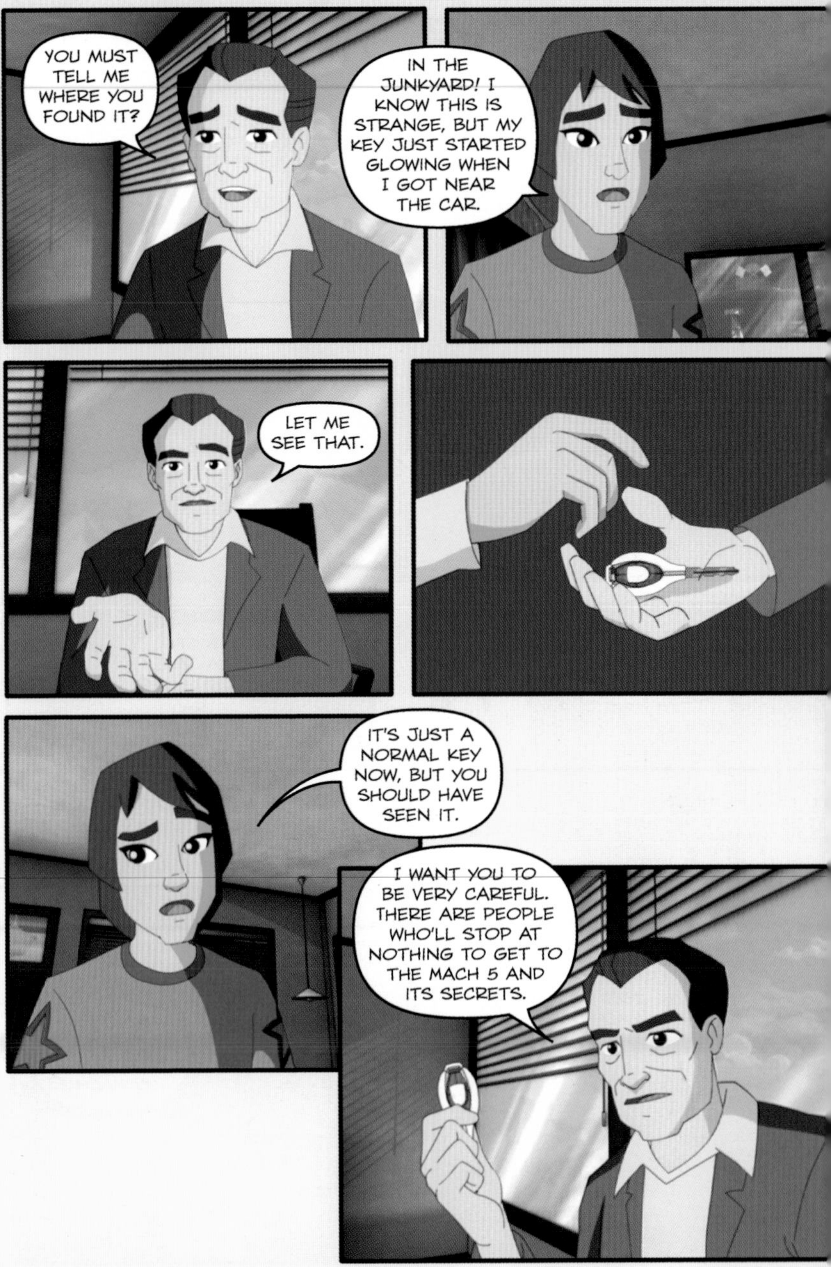
YOU MUST TELL ME WHERE YOU FOUND IT?
IN THE JUNKYARD! I KNOW THIS IS STRANGE, BUT MY KEY JUST STARTED GLOWING WHEN I GOT NEAR THE CAR.
LET ME SEE THAT.
IT'S JUST A NORMAL KEY NOW, BUT YOU SHOULD HAVE SEEN IT.
I WANT YOU TO BE VERY CAREFUL. THERE ARE PEOPLE WHO'LL STOP AT NOTHING TO GET TO THE MACH 5 AND ITS SECRETS.

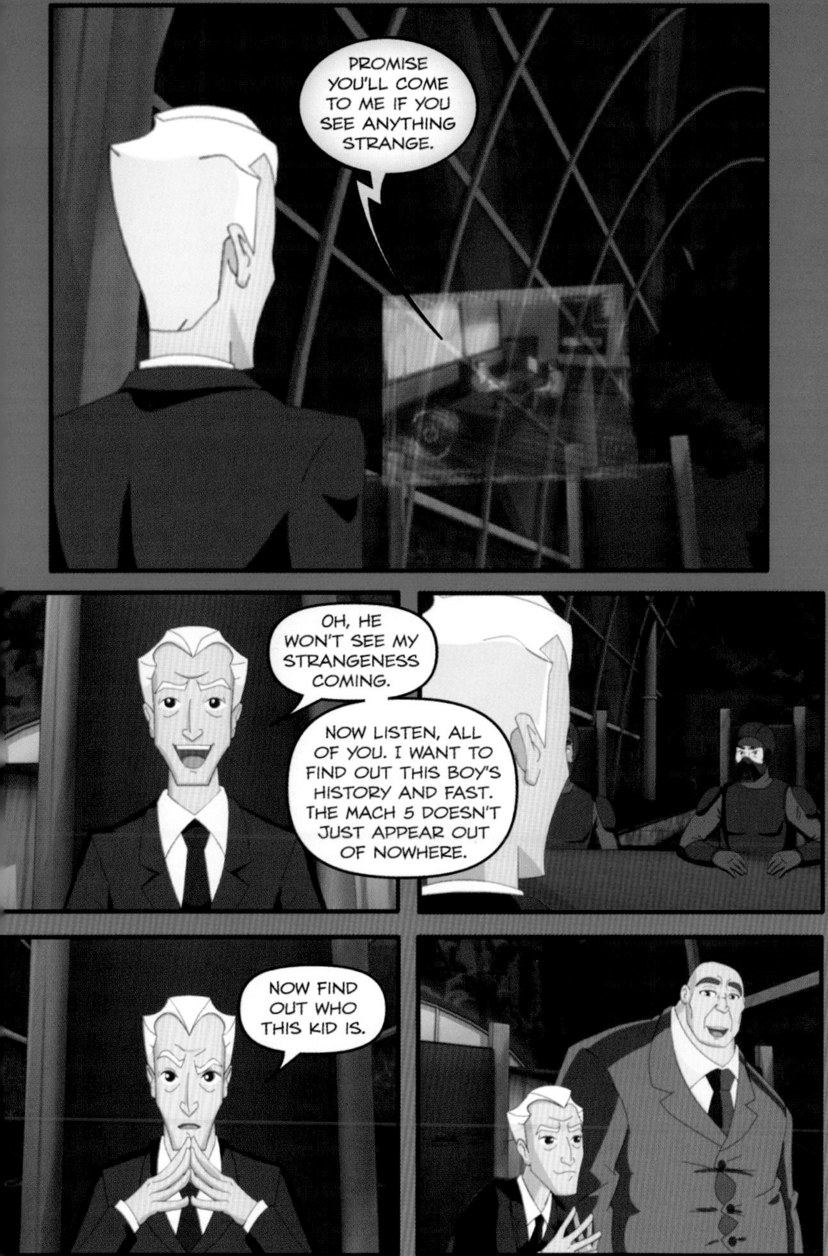
PROMISE YOU'LL COME TO ME IF YOU SEE ANYTHING STRANGE.
OH, HE WON'T SEE MY STRANGENESS COMING.
NOW LISTEN, ALL OF YOU. I WANT TO FIND OUT THIS BOY'S HISTORY AND FAST. THE MACH 5 DOESN'T JUST APPEAR OUT OF NOWHERE.
NOW FIND OUT WHO THIS KID IS.

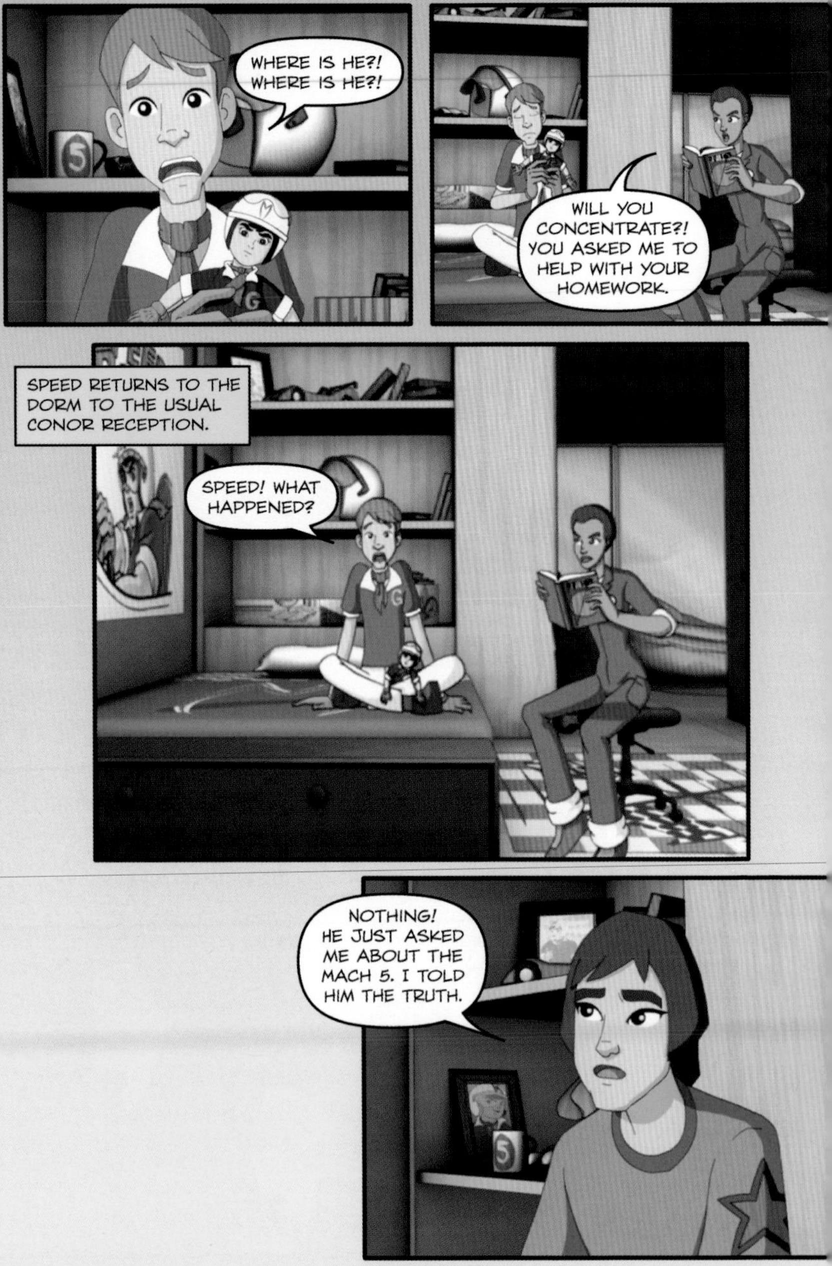
WHERE IS HE?! WHERE IS HE?!
WILL YOU CONCENTRATE?! YOU ASKED ME TO HELP WITH YOUR HOMEWORK.
SPEED RETURNS TO THE DORM TO THE USUAL CONOR RECEPTION.
SPEED! WHAT HAPPENED?
NOTHING! HE JUST ASKED ME ABOUT THE MACH 5. I TOLD HIM THE TRUTH.

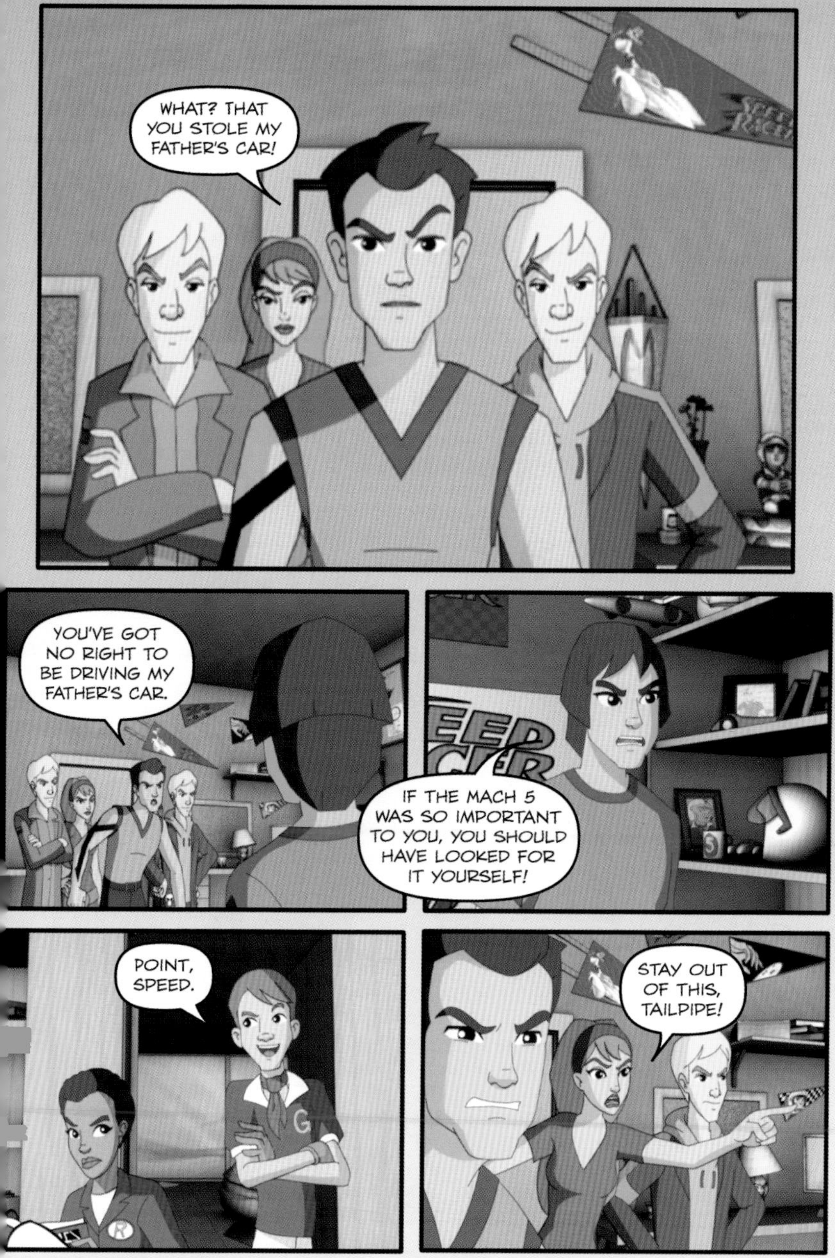

WHAT? THAT YOU STOLE MY FATHER'S CAR!
YOU'VE GOT NO RIGHT TO BE DRIVING MY FATHER'S CAR.
IF THE MACH 5 WAS SO IMPORTANT TO YOU, YOU SHOULD HAVE LOOKED FOR IT YOURSELF!
POINT, SPEED.
STAY OUT OF THIS, TAILPIPE!

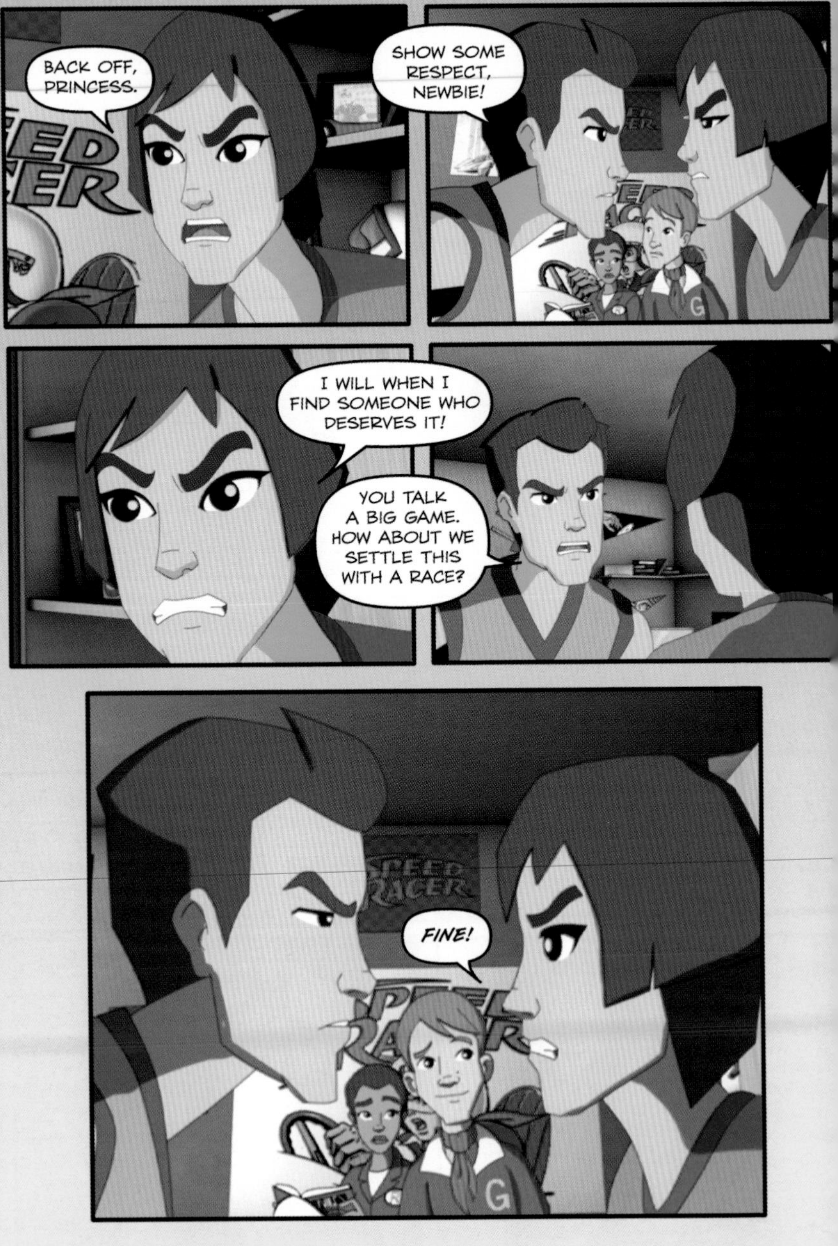
BACK OFF, PRINCESS.
SHOW SOME RESPECT, NEWBIE!
I WILL WHEN I FIND SOMEONE WHO DESERVES IT!
YOU TALK A BIG GAME. HOW ABOUT WE SETTLE THIS WITH A RACE?
FINE!

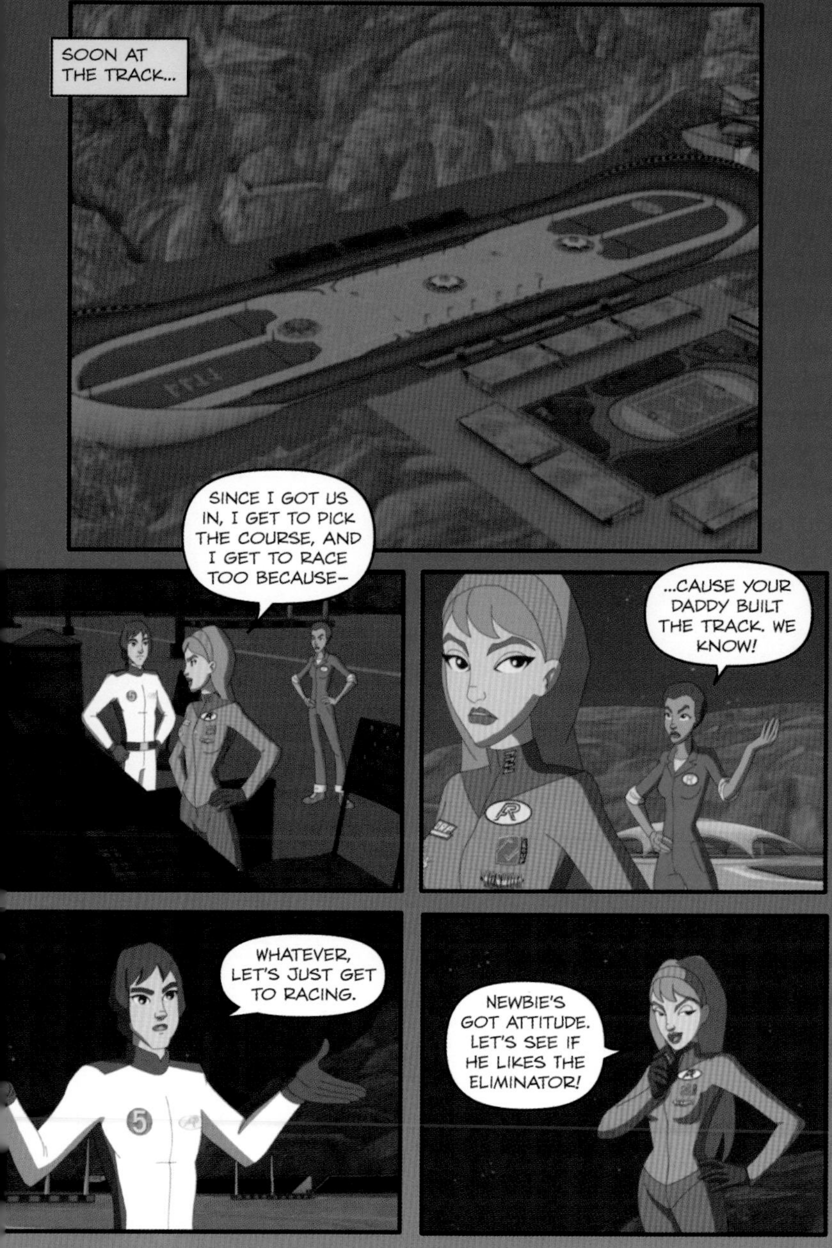
SOON AT THE TRACK...
SINCE I GOT US IN, I GET TO PICK THE COURSE, AND I GET TO RACE TOO BECAUSE–
...CAUSE YOUR DADDY BUILT THE TRACK. WE KNOW!
WHATEVER, LET'S JUST GET TO RACING.
NEWBIE'S GOT ATTITUDE. LET'S SEE IF HE LIKES THE ELIMINATOR!

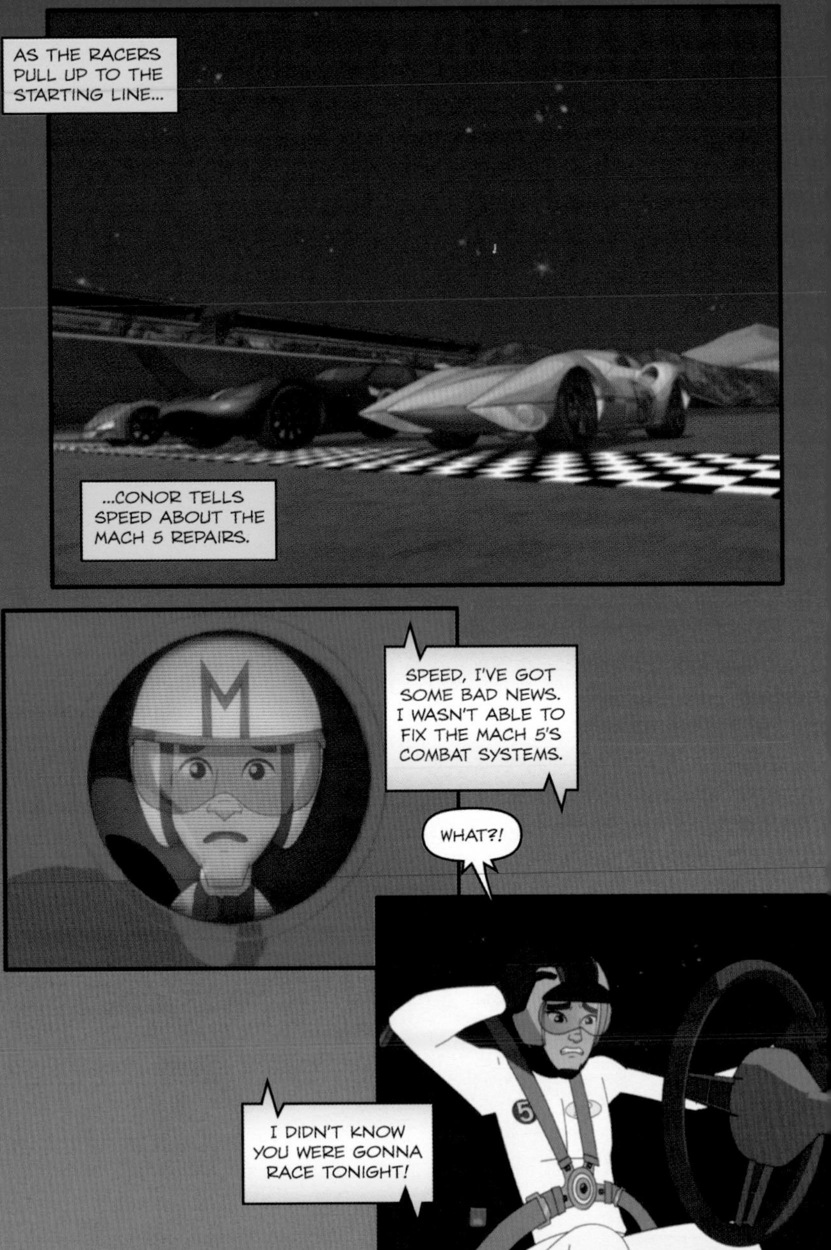

AS THE RACERS PULL UP TO THE STARTING LINE...
...CONOR TELLS SPEED ABOUT THE MACH 5 REPAIRS.
SPEED, I'VE GOT SOME BAD NEWS. I WASN'T ABLE TO FIX THE MACH 5'S COMBAT SYSTEMS.
WHAT?!
I DIDN'T KNOW YOU WERE GONNA RACE TONIGHT!

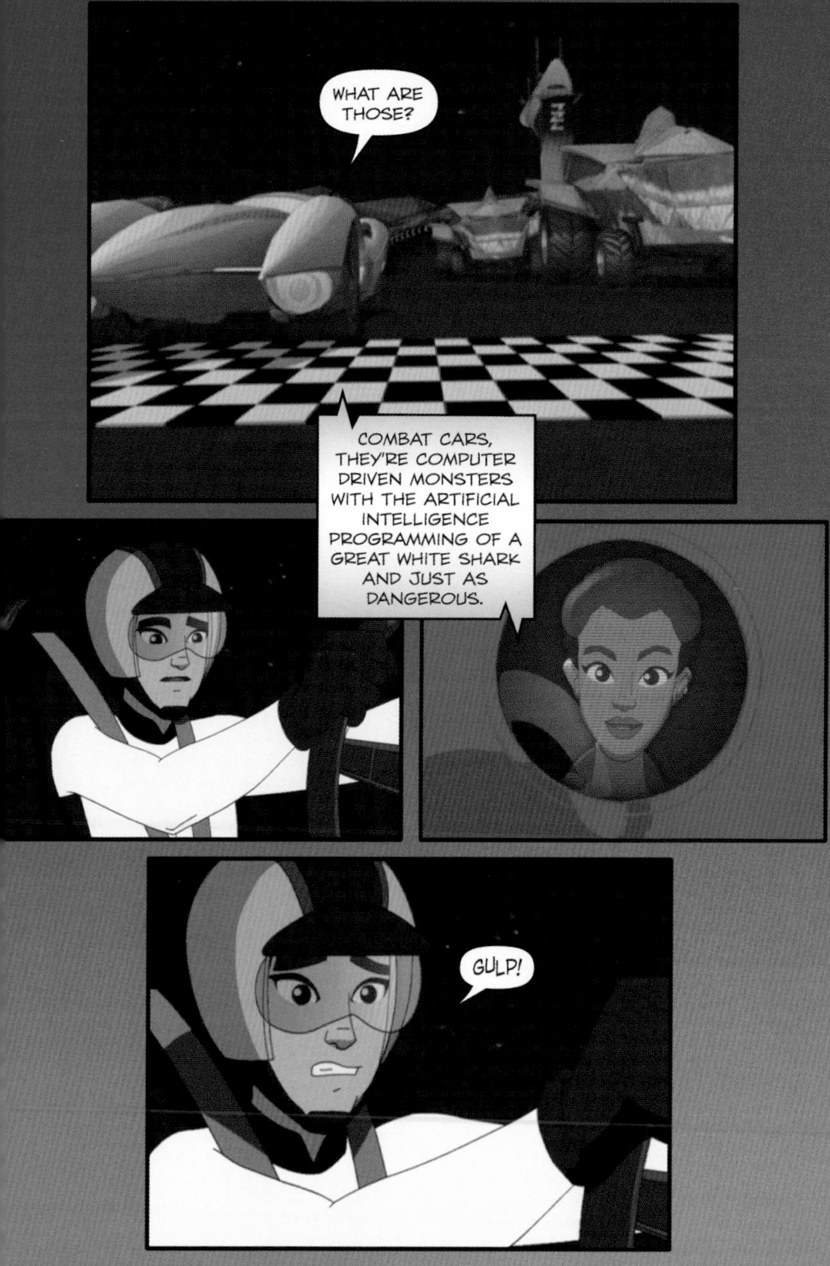
WHAT ARE THOSE?
COMBAT CARS, THEY'RE COMPUTER DRIVEN MONSTERS WITH THE ARTIFICIAL INTELLIGENCE PROGRAMMING OF A GREAT WHITE SHARK AND JUST AS DANGEROUS.
GULP!

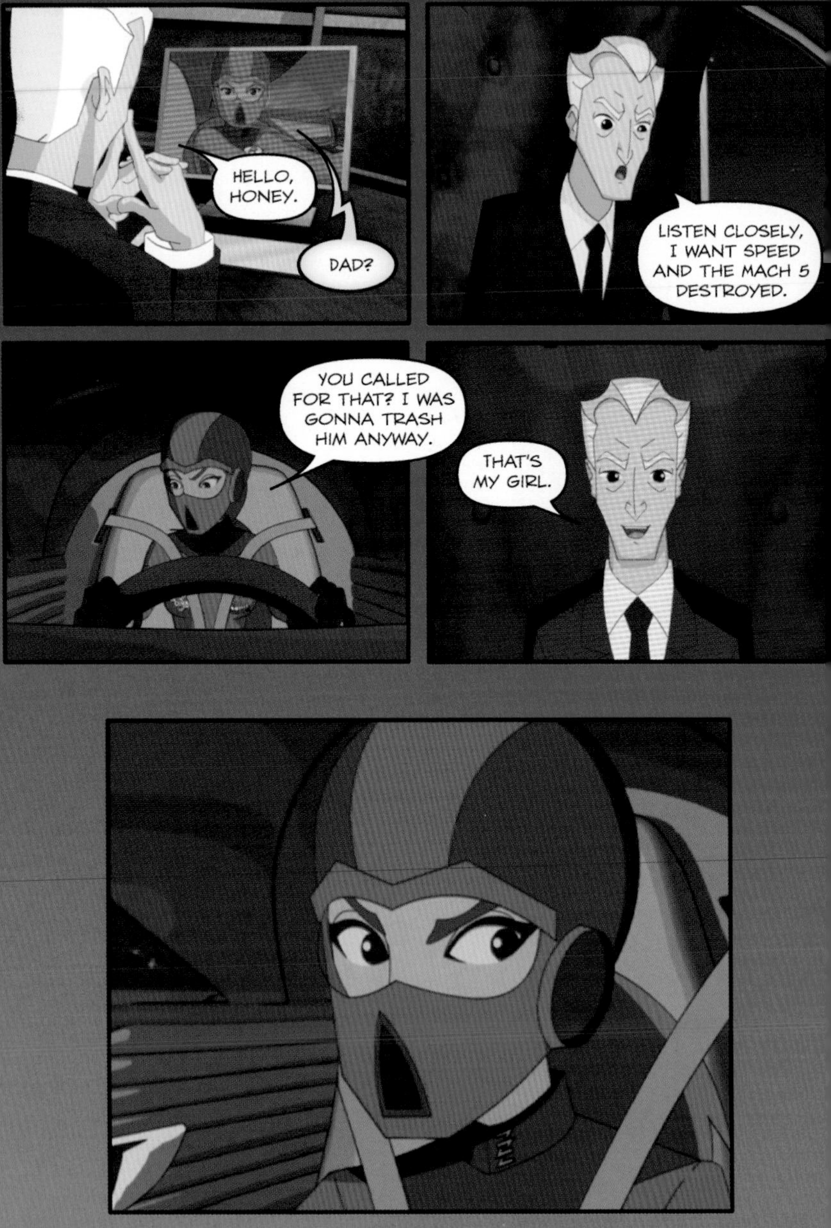
HELLO, HONEY.
DAD?
LISTEN CLOSELY, I WANT SPEED AND THE MACH 5 DESTROYED.
YOU CALLED FOR THAT? I WAS GONNA TRASH HIM ANYWAY.
THAT'S MY GIRL.

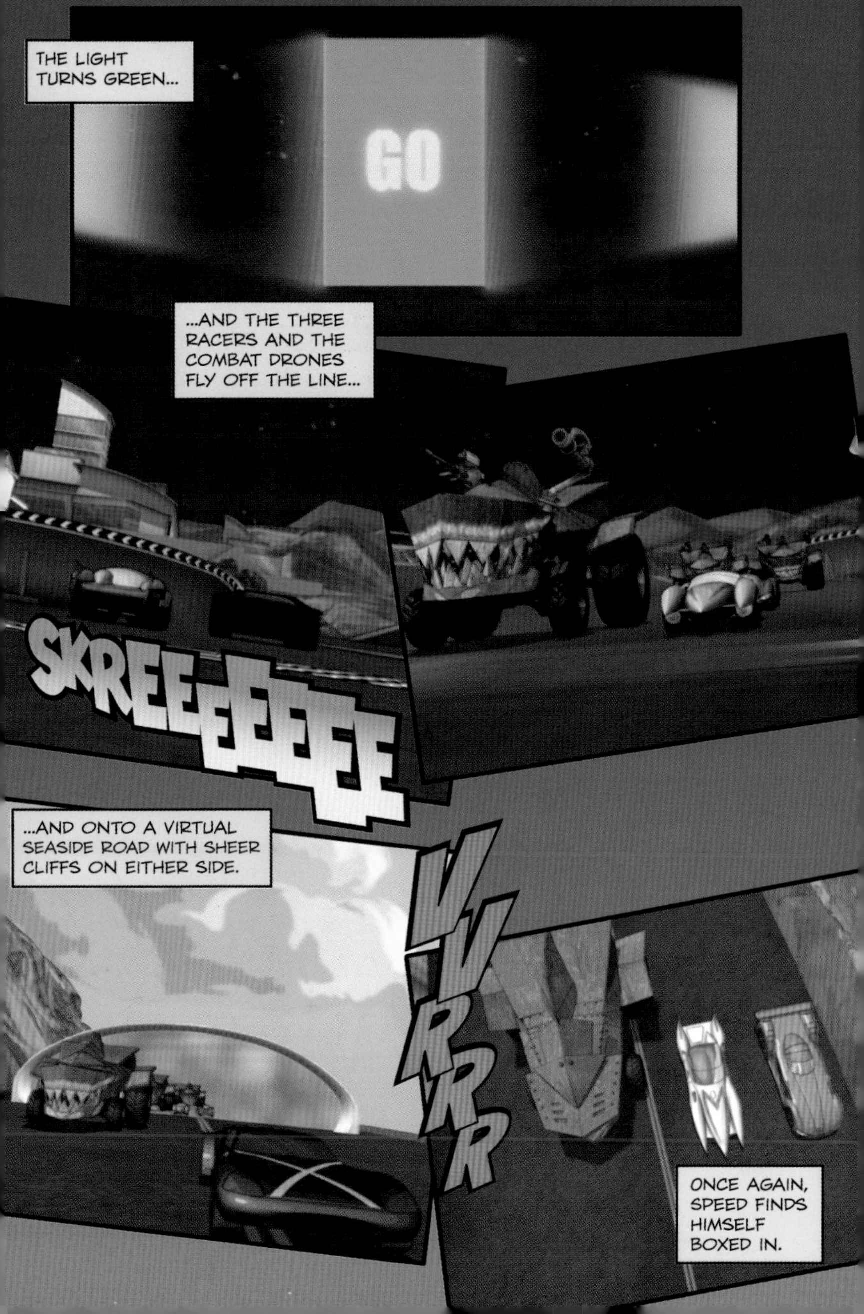
THE LIGHT TURNS GREEN...
GO
...AND THE THREE RACERS AND THE COMBAT DRONES FLY OFF THE LINE...
SKREEEEEEEE
...AND ONTO A VIRTUAL SEASIDE ROAD WITH SHEER CLIFFS ON EITHER SIDE.
VVRRR
ONCE AGAIN, SPEED FINDS HIMSELF BOXED IN.

DO IT! DO IT *NOW!*

ZAZIC'S GREED GETS THE BETTER OF HIM, AS HE ORDERS HIS DAUGHTER INTO DIRECT DANGER.

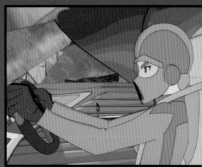

IT'S TOO SOON.

I SAID *NOW!*

FWOOSH

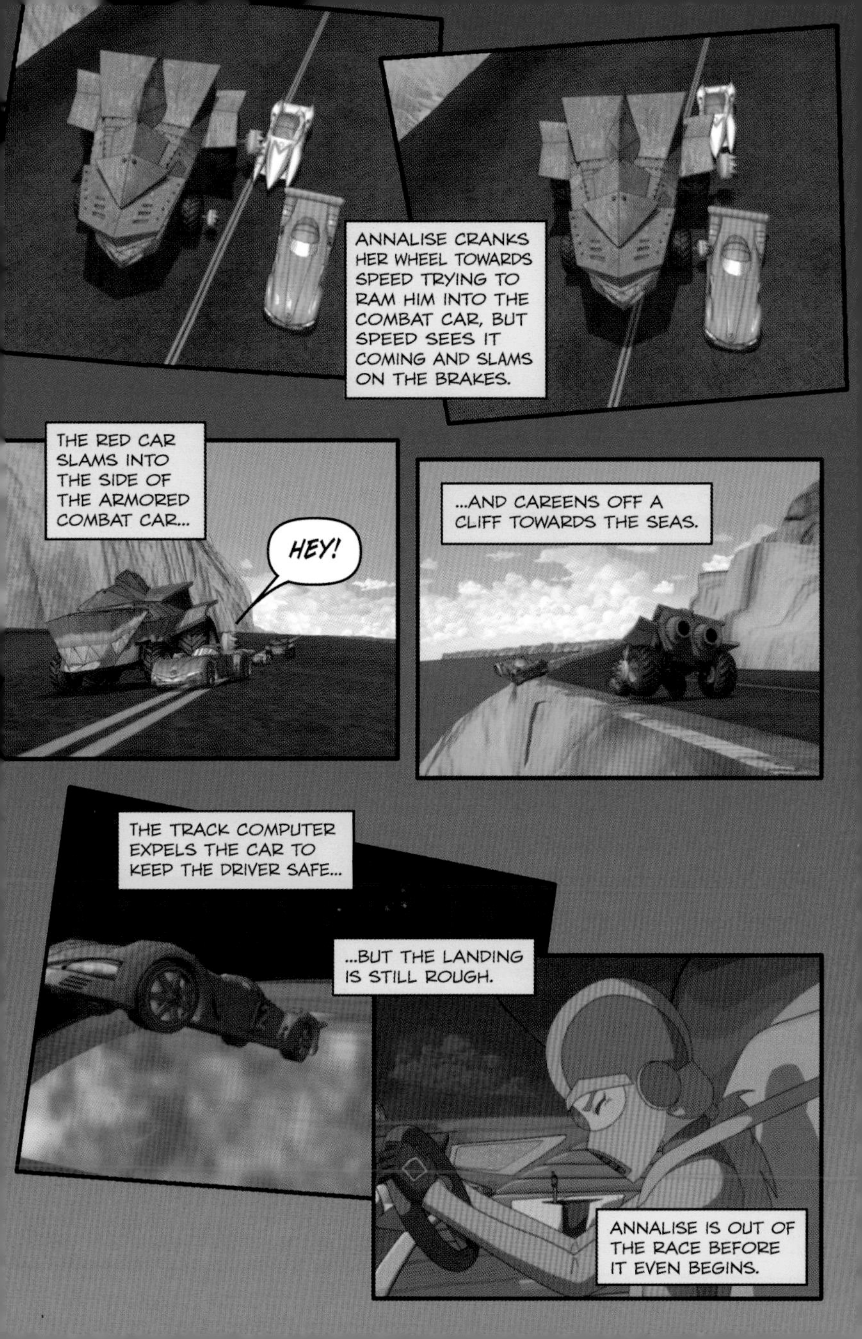
ANNALISE CRANKS HER WHEEL TOWARDS SPEED TRYING TO RAM HIM INTO THE COMBAT CAR, BUT SPEED SEES IT COMING AND SLAMS ON THE BRAKES.
THE RED CAR SLAMS INTO THE SIDE OF THE ARMORED COMBAT CAR...
HEY!
...AND CAREENS OFF A CLIFF TOWARDS THE SEAS.
THE TRACK COMPUTER EXPELS THE CAR TO KEEP THE DRIVER SAFE...
...BUT THE LANDING IS STILL ROUGH.
ANNALISE IS OUT OF THE RACE BEFORE IT EVEN BEGINS.

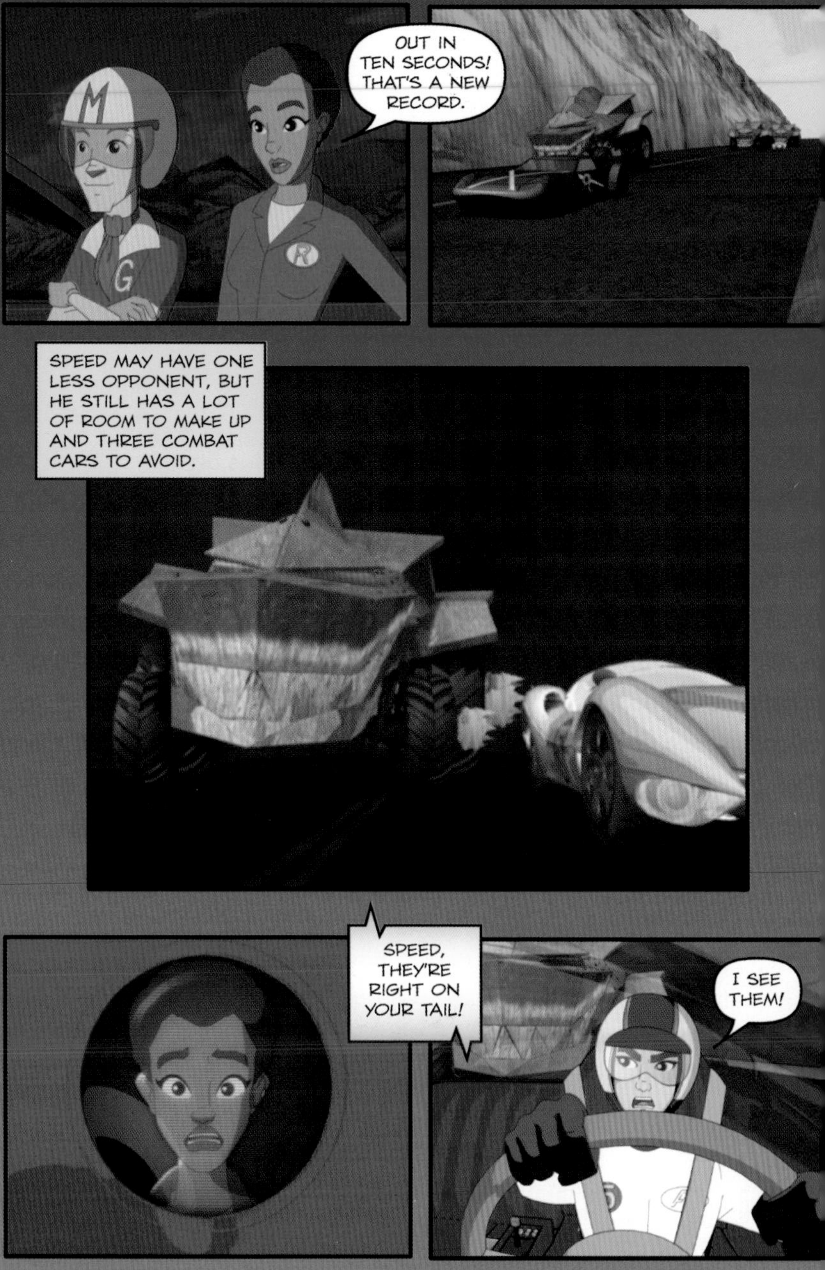
OUT IN TEN SECONDS! THAT'S A NEW RECORD.
SPEED MAY HAVE ONE LESS OPPONENT, BUT HE STILL HAS A LOT OF ROOM TO MAKE UP AND THREE COMBAT CARS TO AVOID.
SPEED, THEY'RE RIGHT ON YOUR TAIL!
I SEE THEM!

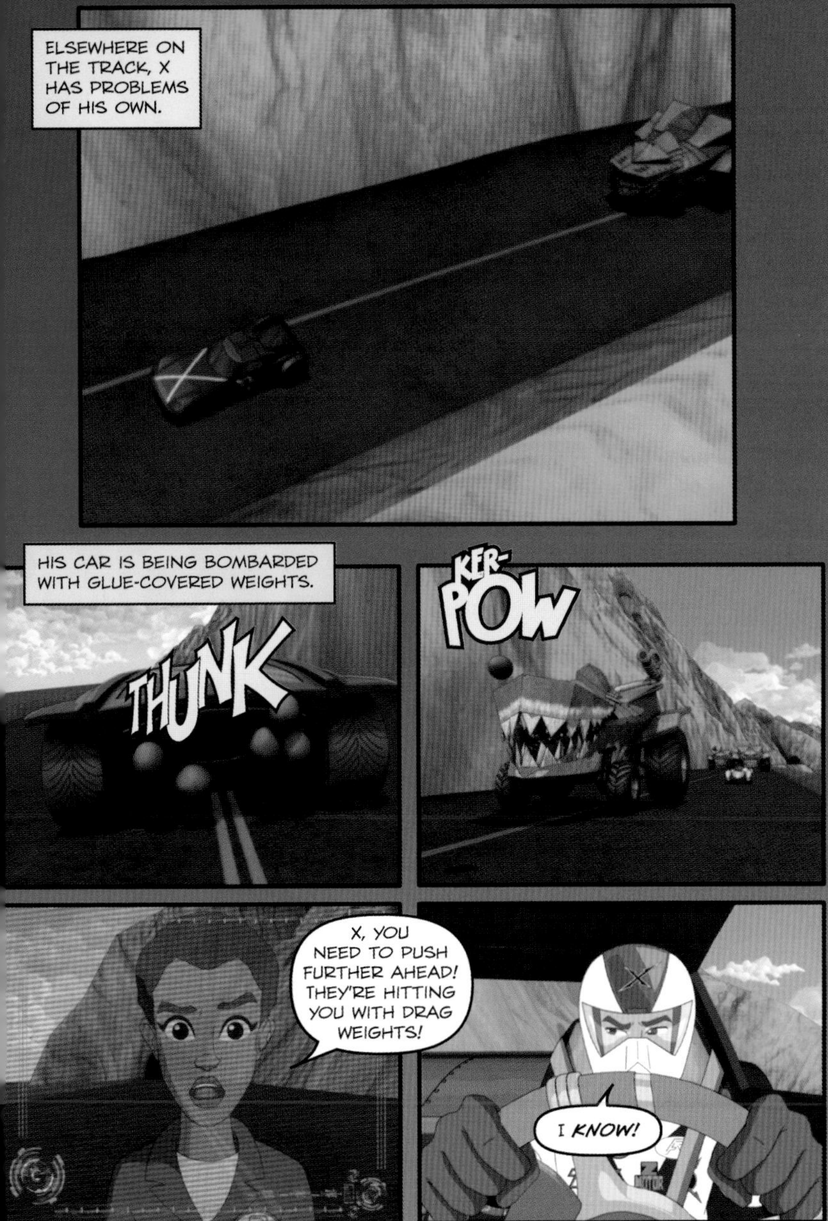
ELSEWHERE ON THE TRACK, X HAS PROBLEMS OF HIS OWN.
HIS CAR IS BEING BOMBARDED WITH GLUE-COVERED WEIGHTS.
THUNK
KER-POW
X, YOU NEED TO PUSH FURTHER AHEAD! THEY'RE HITTING YOU WITH DRAG WEIGHTS!
I KNOW!

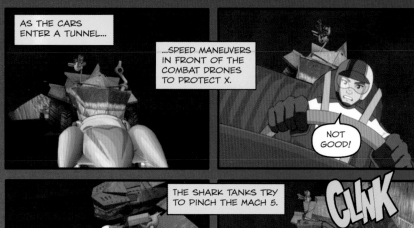

AS THE CARS ENTER A TUNNEL...

...SPEED MANEUVERS IN FRONT OF THE COMBAT DRONES TO PROTECT X.

NOT GOOD!

THE SHARK TANKS TRY TO PINCH THE MACH 5.

CLINK
CLINK
CLINK

NO MATTER WHAT SPEED DOES THE DRONES HAVE AN ANSWER.

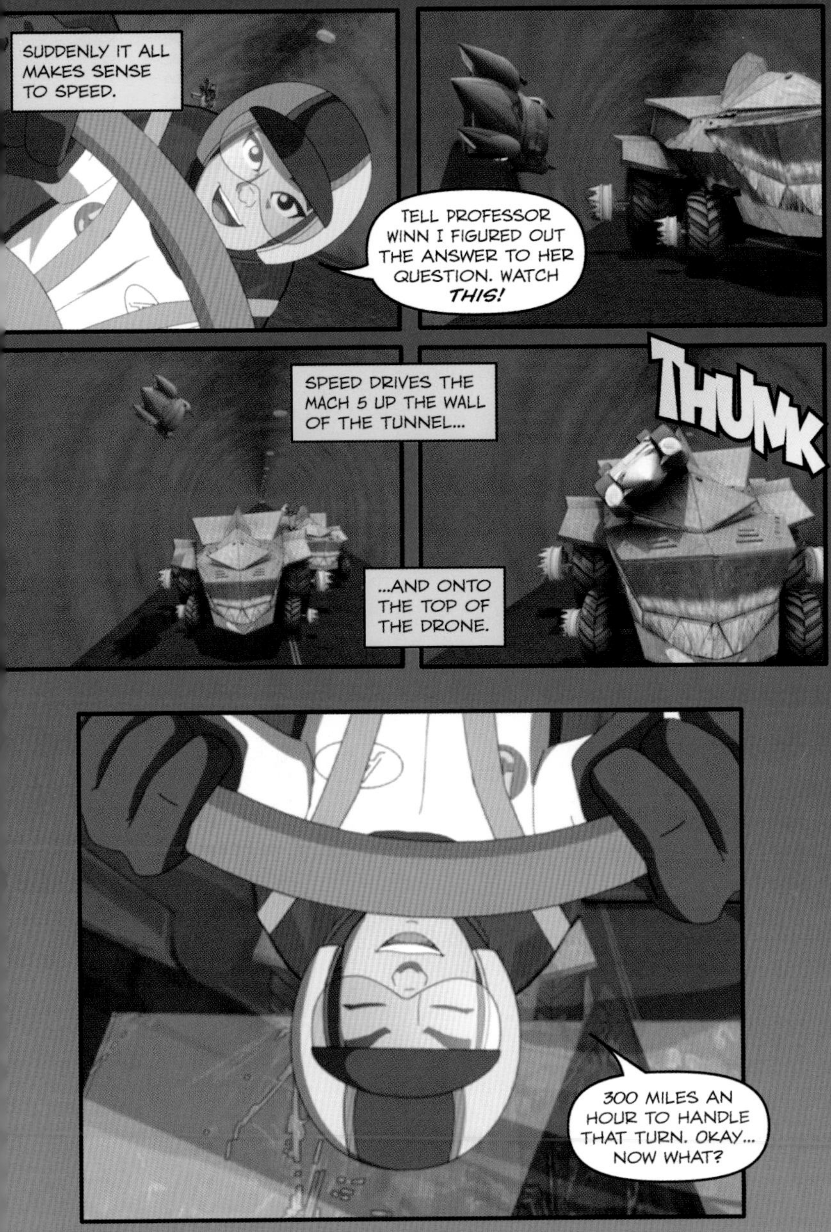
SUDDENLY IT ALL MAKES SENSE TO SPEED.
TELL PROFESSOR WINN I FIGURED OUT THE ANSWER TO HER QUESTION. WATCH THIS!
SPEED DRIVES THE MACH 5 UP THE WALL OF THE TUNNEL...
THUNK
...AND ONTO THE TOP OF THE DRONE.
300 MILES AN HOUR TO HANDLE THAT TURN. OKAY... NOW WHAT?

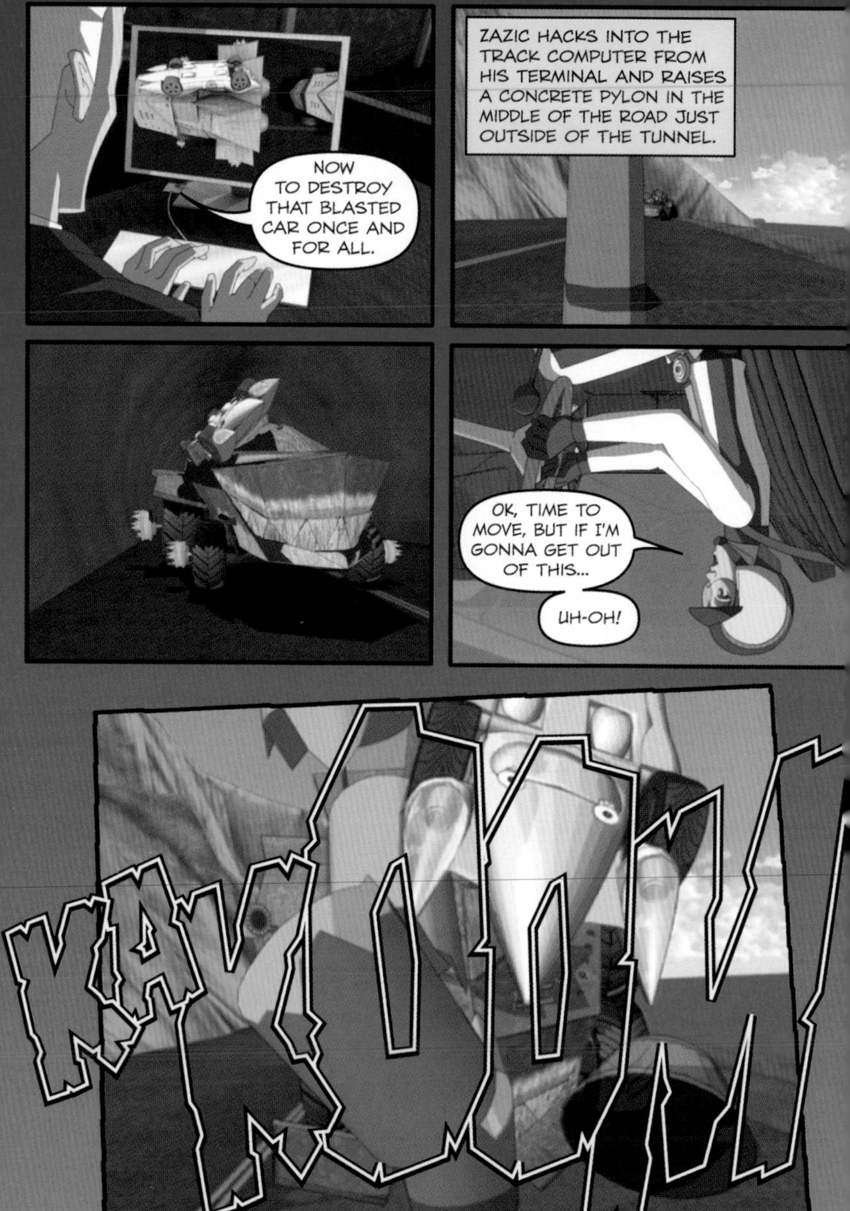
NOW TO DESTROY THAT BLASTED CAR ONCE AND FOR ALL.
ZAZIC HACKS INTO THE TRACK COMPUTER FROM HIS TERMINAL AND RAISES A CONCRETE PYLON IN THE MIDDLE OF THE ROAD JUST OUTSIDE OF THE TUNNEL.
OK, TIME TO MOVE, BUT IF I'M GONNA GET OUT OF THIS...
UH-OH!
KAVROOOM

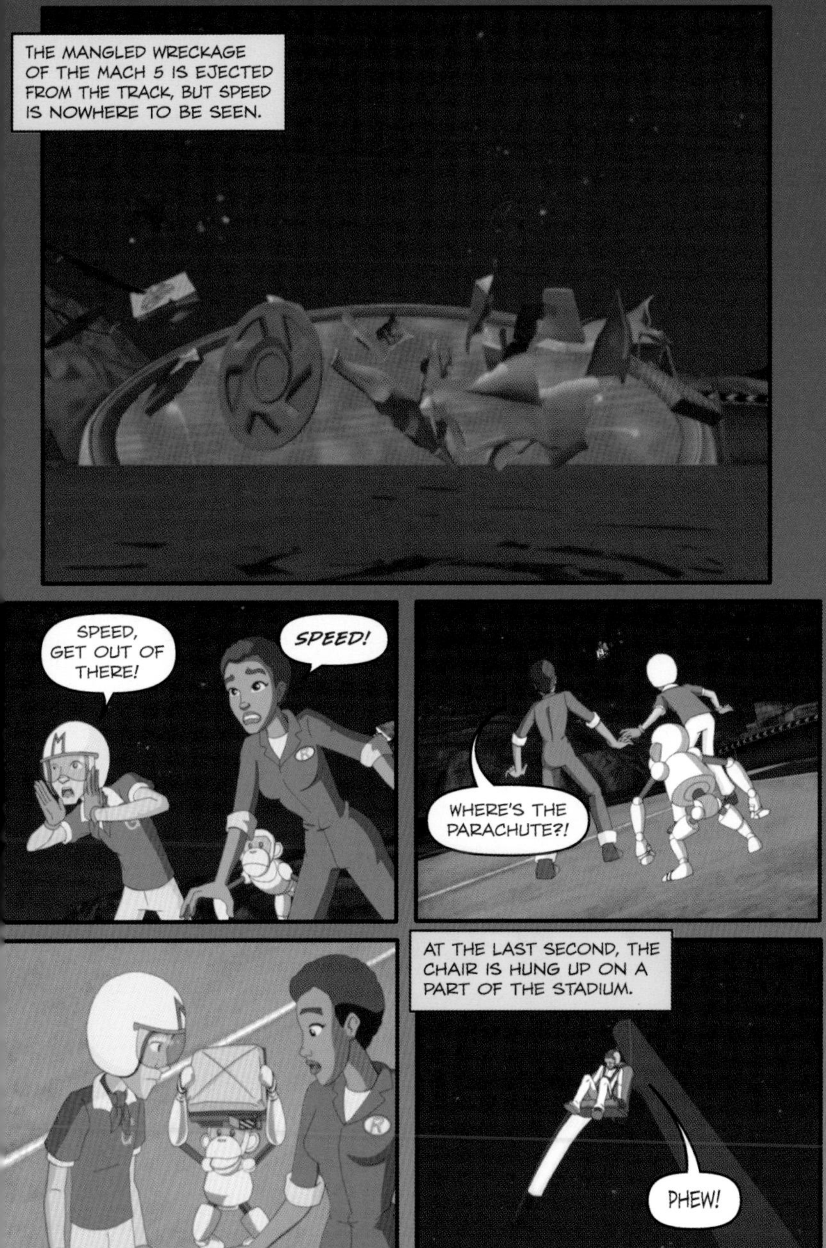
THE MANGLED WRECKAGE OF THE MACH 5 IS EJECTED FROM THE TRACK, BUT SPEED IS NOWHERE TO BE SEEN.
SPEED, GET OUT OF THERE!
SPEED!
WHERE'S THE PARACHUTE?!
AT THE LAST SECOND, THE CHAIR IS HUNG UP ON A PART OF THE STADIUM.
PHEW!

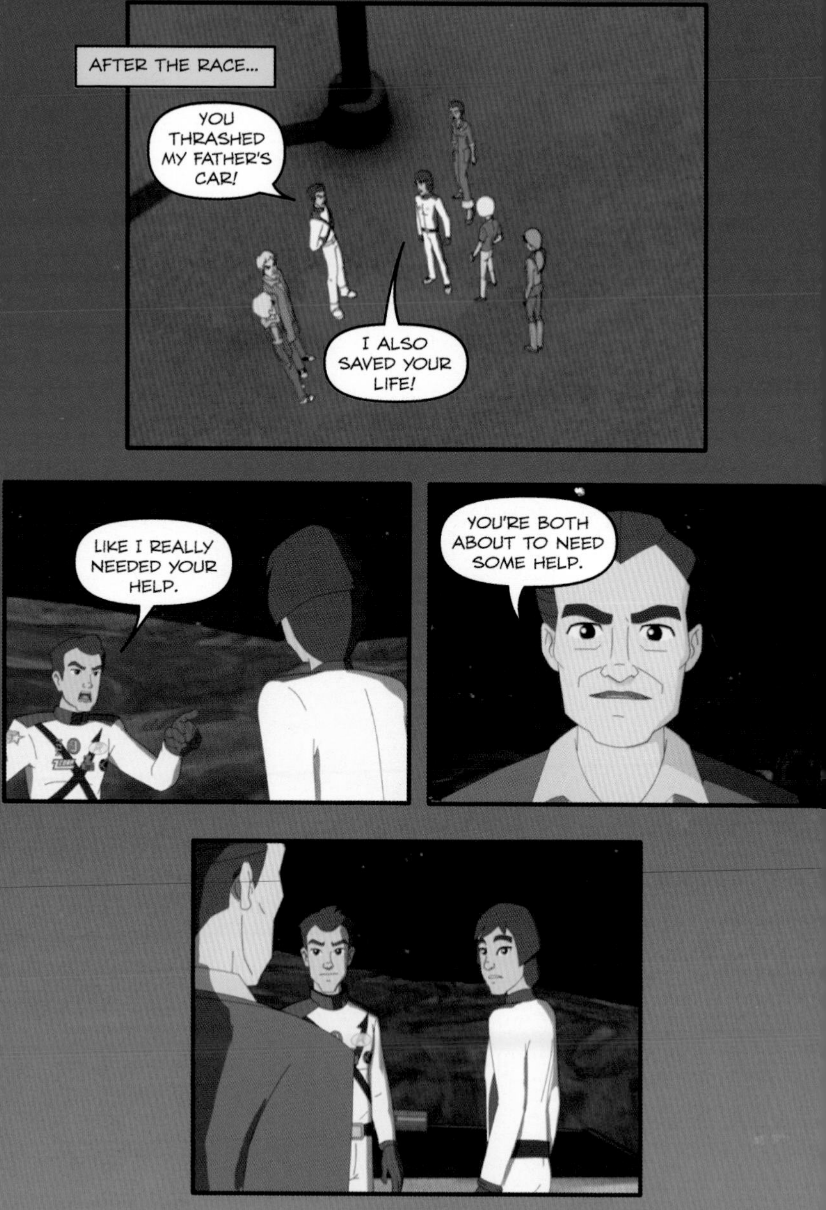
AFTER THE RACE...
YOU THRASHED MY FATHER'S CAR!
I ALSO SAVED YOUR LIFE!
LIKE I REALLY NEEDED YOUR HELP.
YOU'RE BOTH ABOUT TO NEED SOME HELP.

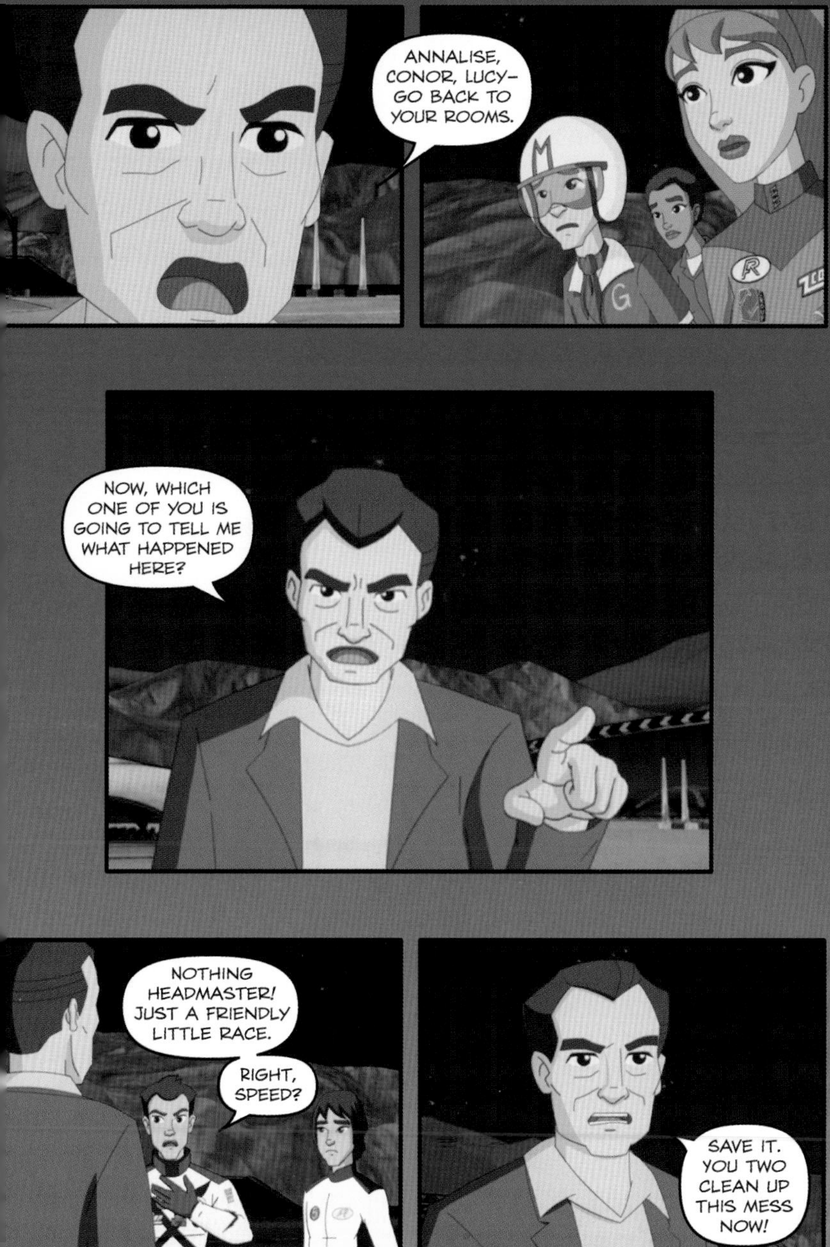
ANNALISE, CONOR, LUCY– GO BACK TO YOUR ROOMS.
NOW, WHICH ONE OF YOU IS GOING TO TELL ME WHAT HAPPENED HERE?
NOTHING HEADMASTER! JUST A FRIENDLY LITTLE RACE.
RIGHT, SPEED?
SAVE IT. YOU TWO CLEAN UP THIS MESS NOW!

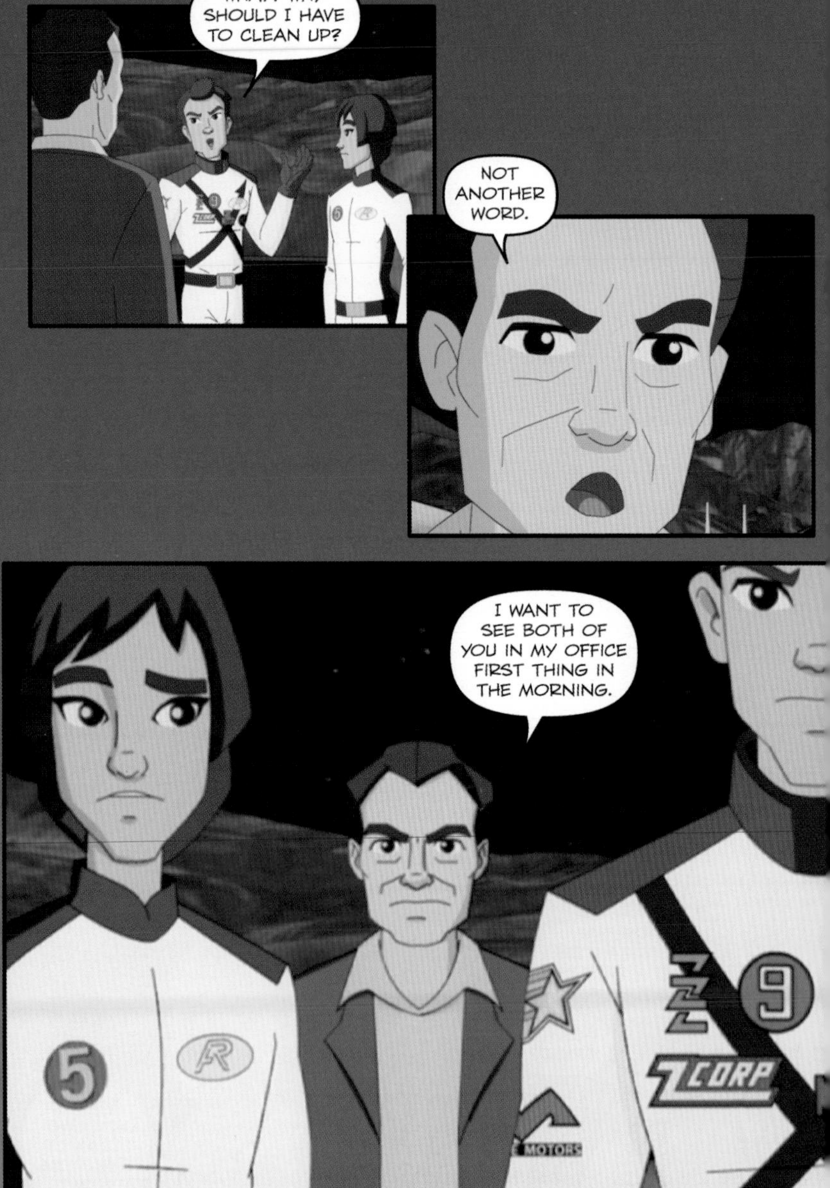
WHAT? WHY SHOULD I HAVE TO CLEAN UP?
NOT ANOTHER WORD.
I WANT TO SEE BOTH OF YOU IN MY OFFICE FIRST THING IN THE MORNING.

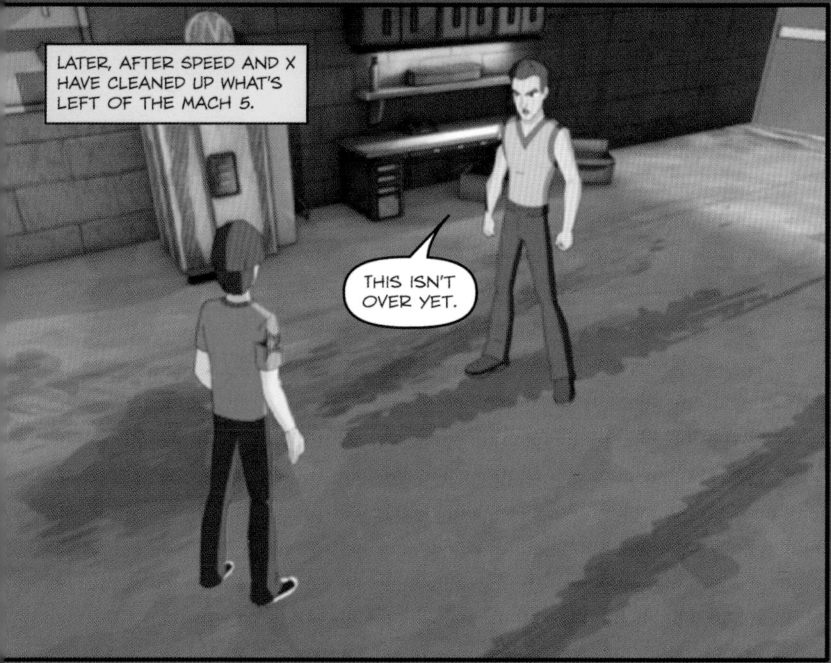
LATER, AFTER SPEED AND X HAVE CLEANED UP WHAT'S LEFT OF THE MACH 5.
THIS ISN'T OVER YET.

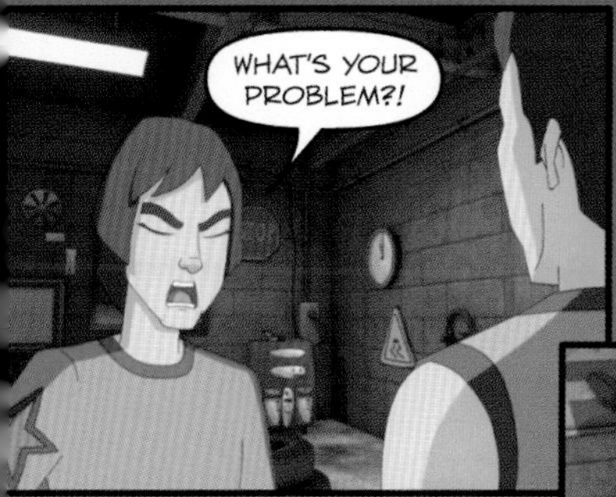
WHAT'S YOUR PROBLEM?!

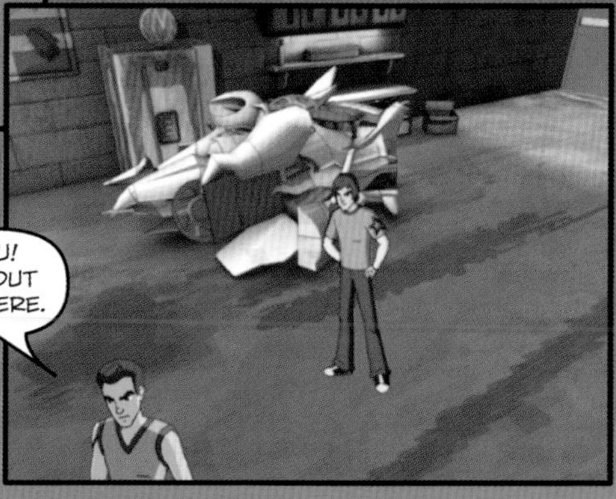
YOU! I'M OUT OF HERE.

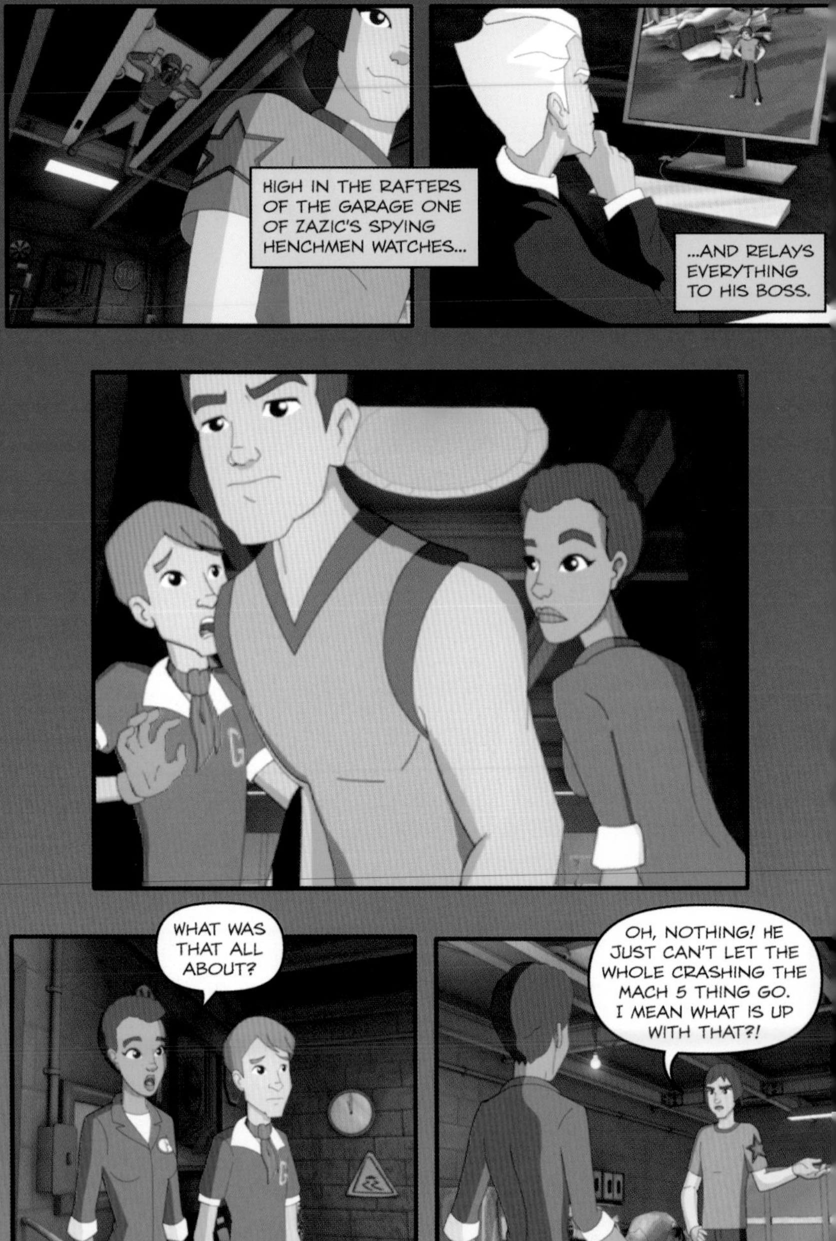
HIGH IN THE RAFTERS OF THE GARAGE ONE OF ZAZIC'S SPYING HENCHMEN WATCHES...
...AND RELAYS EVERYTHING TO HIS BOSS.
WHAT WAS THAT ALL ABOUT?
OH, NOTHING! HE JUST CAN'T LET THE WHOLE CRASHING THE MACH 5 THING GO. I MEAN WHAT IS UP WITH THAT?!

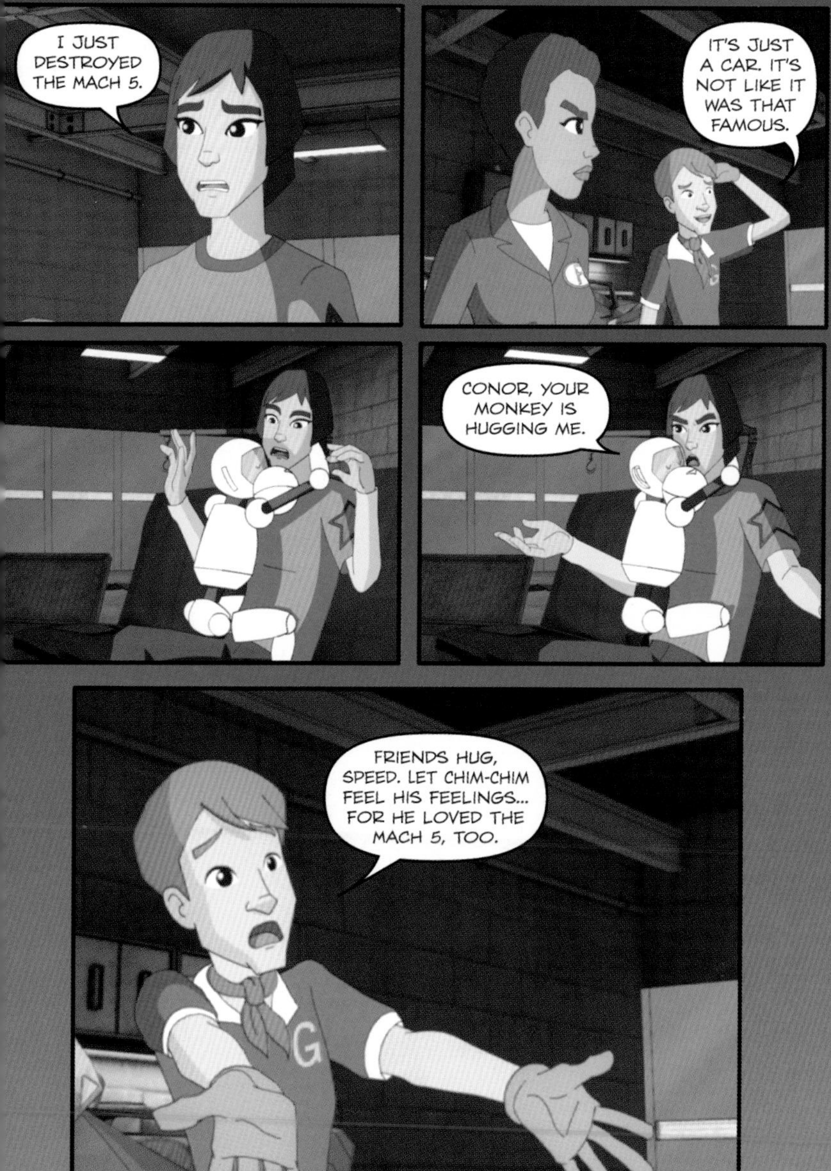
I JUST DESTROYED THE MACH 5.
IT'S JUST A CAR. IT'S NOT LIKE IT WAS THAT FAMOUS.
CONOR, YOUR MONKEY IS HUGGING ME.
FRIENDS HUG, SPEED. LET CHIM-CHIM FEEL HIS FEELINGS... FOR HE LOVED THE MACH 5, TOO.

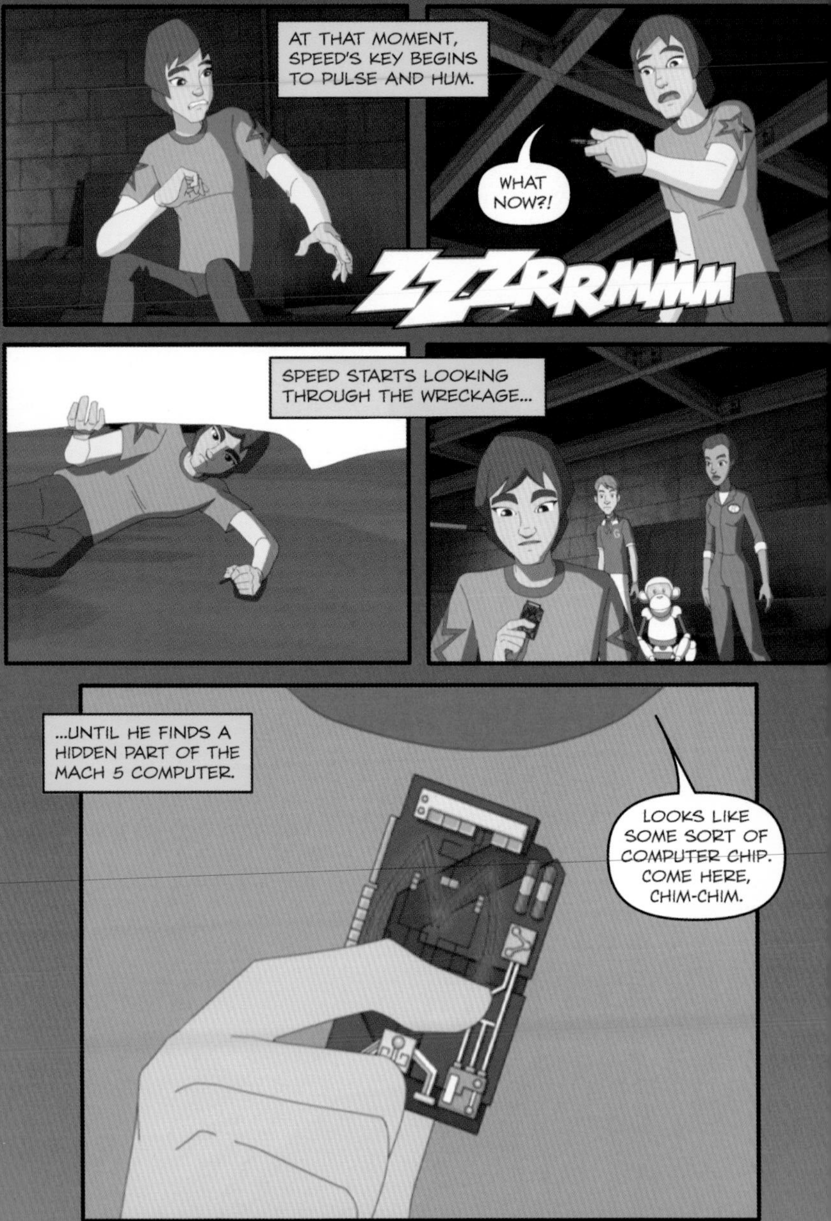
AT THAT MOMENT, SPEED'S KEY BEGINS TO PULSE AND HUM.
WHAT NOW?!
ZZZRRMMMM
SPEED STARTS LOOKING THROUGH THE WRECKAGE...
...UNTIL HE FINDS A HIDDEN PART OF THE MACH 5 COMPUTER.
LOOKS LIKE SOME SORT OF COMPUTER CHIP. COME HERE, CHIM-CHIM.

SPEED PLACES THE CHIP INTO CHIM-CHIM.

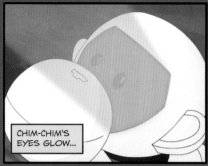

CHIM-CHIM'S EYES GLOW...

...AS HE PROJECTS AN IMAGE OF AN ENGINE INTO THE AIR.

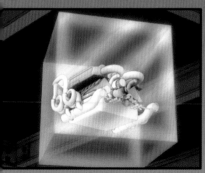

WHOA! IS THAT WHAT I THINK IT IS?

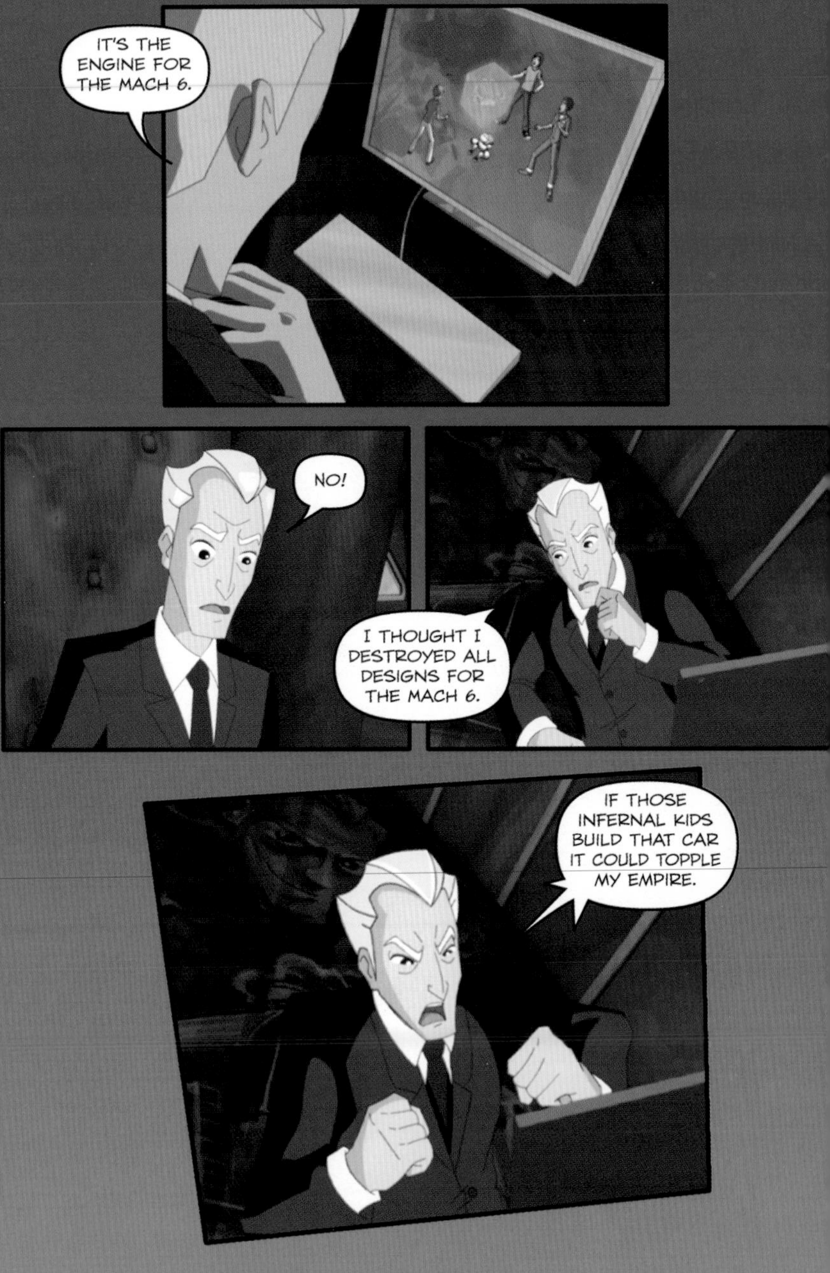
IT'S THE ENGINE FOR THE MACH 6.
NO!
I THOUGHT I DESTROYED ALL DESIGNS FOR THE MACH 6.
IF THOSE INFERNAL KIDS BUILD THAT CAR IT COULD TOPPLE MY EMPIRE.

WE'VE GOT TO BUILD IT!

I HATE TO BE THE FLAT TIRE ON THIS TRICYCLE, BUT THE MACH 5 IS TOTALED AND WE DON'T HAVE THE MONEY OR PARTS TO BUILD A NEW CAR.

NO... NO WAY. WE'RE LOOKING AT THE MOST SOPHISTICATED ENGINE EVER DESIGNED. I WANT TO BUILD IT!

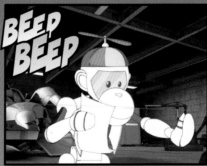

BEEP BEEP

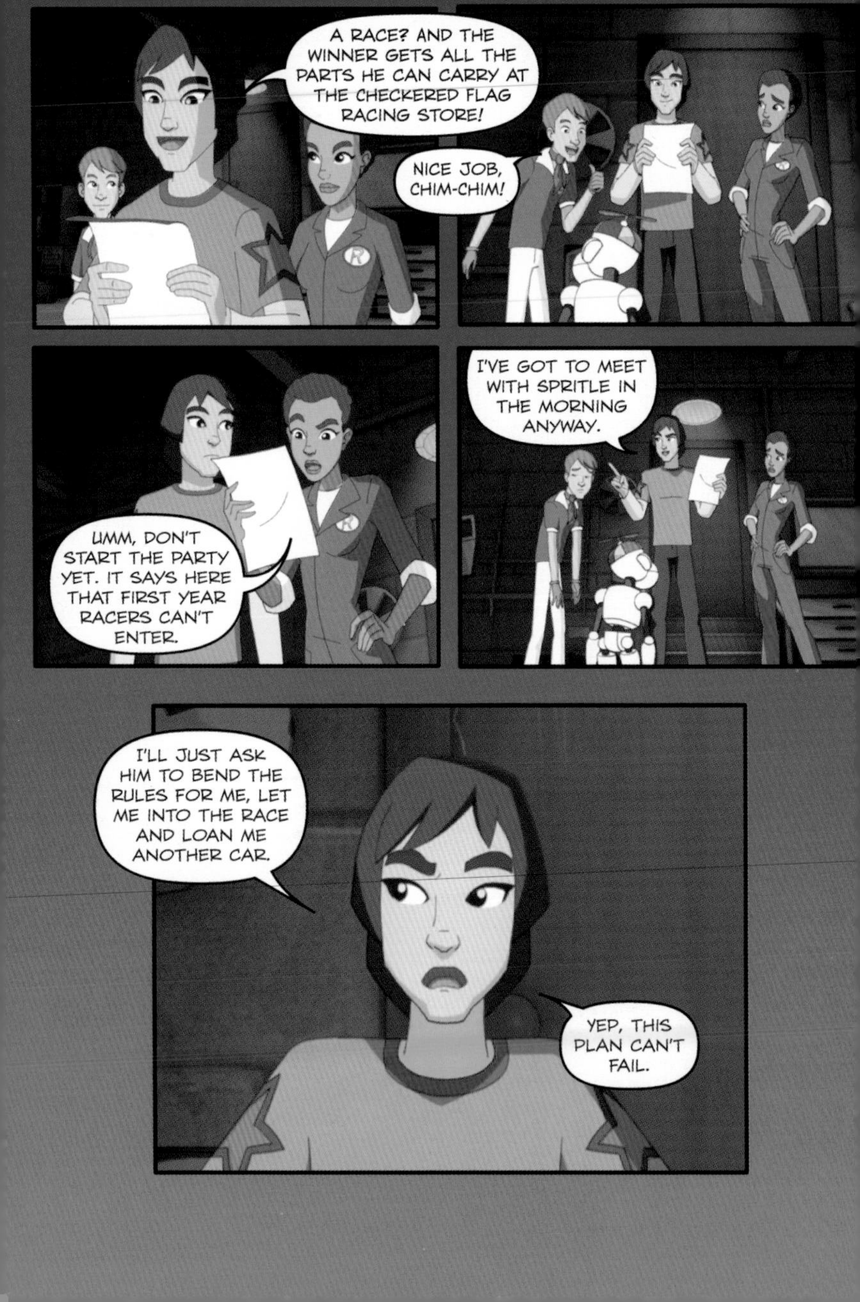
A RACE? AND THE WINNER GETS ALL THE PARTS HE CAN CARRY AT THE CHECKERED FLAG RACING STORE!
NICE JOB, CHIM-CHIM!
UMM, DON'T START THE PARTY YET. IT SAYS HERE THAT FIRST YEAR RACERS CAN'T ENTER.
I'VE GOT TO MEET WITH SPRITLE IN THE MORNING ANYWAY.
I'LL JUST ASK HIM TO BEND THE RULES FOR ME, LET ME INTO THE RACE AND LOAN ME ANOTHER CAR.
YEP, THIS PLAN CAN'T FAIL.

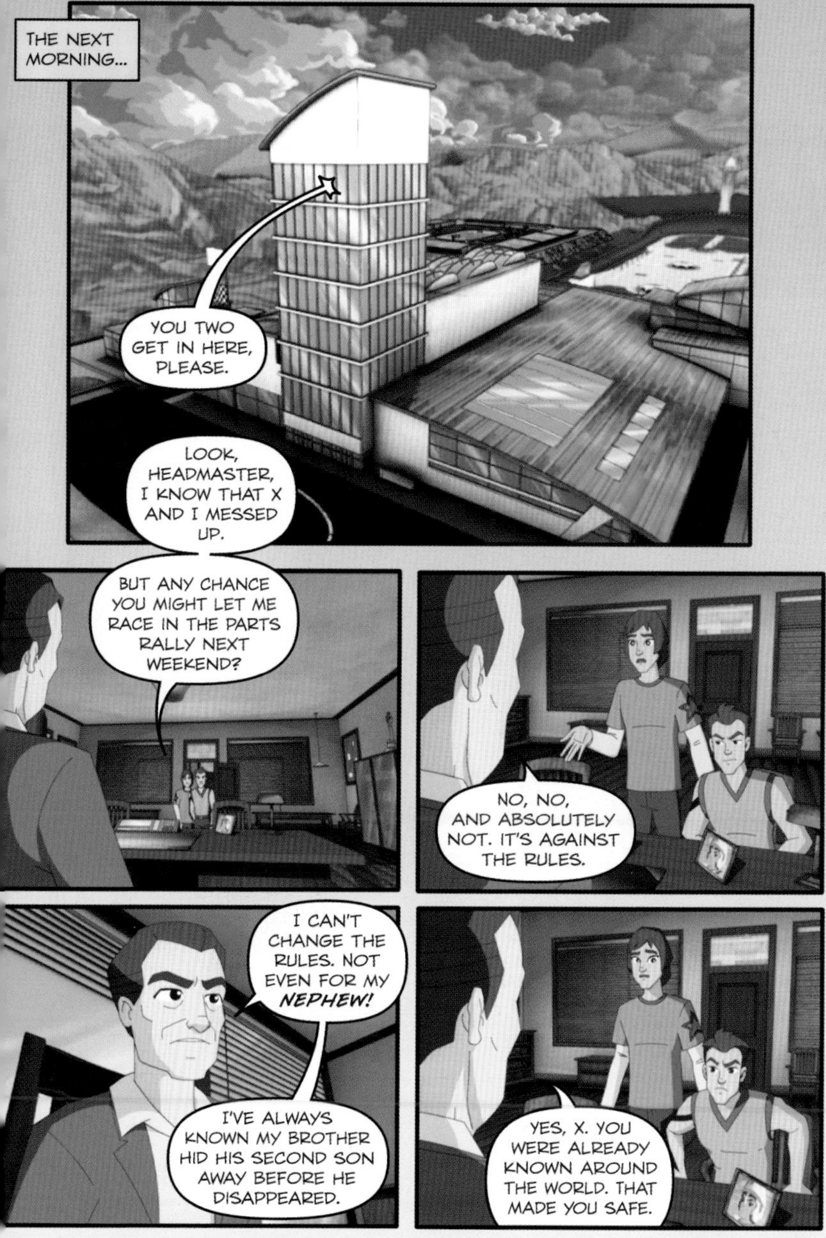
THE NEXT MORNING...
YOU TWO GET IN HERE, PLEASE.
LOOK, HEADMASTER, I KNOW THAT X AND I MESSED UP.
BUT ANY CHANCE YOU MIGHT LET ME RACE IN THE PARTS RALLY NEXT WEEKEND?
NO, NO, AND ABSOLUTELY NOT. IT'S AGAINST THE RULES.
I CAN'T CHANGE THE RULES. NOT EVEN FOR MY NEPHEW!
I'VE ALWAYS KNOWN MY BROTHER HID HIS SECOND SON AWAY BEFORE HE DISAPPEARED.
YES, X. YOU WERE ALREADY KNOWN AROUND THE WORLD. THAT MADE YOU SAFE.

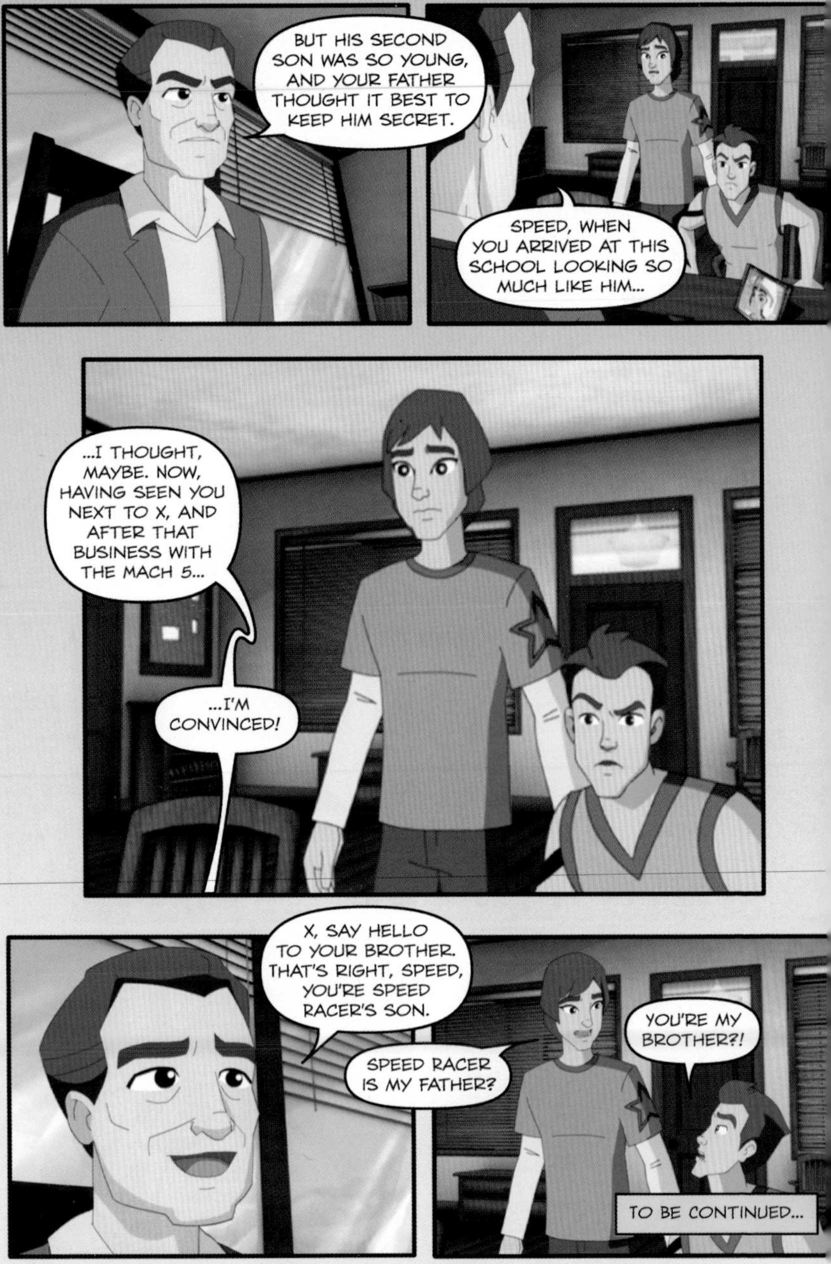
BUT HIS SECOND SON WAS SO YOUNG, AND YOUR FATHER THOUGHT IT BEST TO KEEP HIM SECRET.
SPEED, WHEN YOU ARRIVED AT THIS SCHOOL LOOKING SO MUCH LIKE HIM...
...I THOUGHT, MAYBE. NOW, HAVING SEEN YOU NEXT TO X, AND AFTER THAT BUSINESS WITH THE MACH 5...
...I'M CONVINCED!
X, SAY HELLO TO YOUR BROTHER. THAT'S RIGHT, SPEED, YOU'RE SPEED RACER'S SON.
SPEED RACER IS MY FATHER?
YOU'RE MY BROTHER?!
TO BE CONTINUED...